What If God Kept Score...

It was an ordinary Monday morning, when a 32-year-old milk truck driver entered the West Nickel Mines Amish School at about ten o'clock that morning. It was a simple school that sat along side a country road of Lancaster County, Pennsylvania, filled with the faces of 26 children eager to learn that day's lessons.

The man's name was Charles Carl Roberts. The day was October 2, 2006. Roberts, a father of three, had interrupted the German lesson and asked the class about a clevis pin, a kind of metal fastener, which he said that he had lost on the road. Roberts asked the children, who had just returned from recess, had anyone seen it.

The female teacher replied "no." The teacher had seen Roberts before, as he lived and worked in the area. She offered to allow the class to help him look for it. The children were more than willing to help. Without another word, Roberts left the building and returned to his truck.

Five minutes later, armed with four hundred rounds of ammunition and a semi-automatic

1

weapon, he returned to the schoolhouse. What happened next would change the lives of everyone in that schoolhouse that day.

Within minutes, Roberts dismissed the boys, and other adults from the room. Roberts was then alone to barricade himself in the school with the last of the children, ten little girls, ages 6 to 13. Roberts then began a lesson that no child should ever have to learn.

Charles Roberts ordered the girls to lie down on the floor, facing the blackboard. He, then, tied the hands and feet of each of the girls. Fearing the worst, the oldest of the girls, at only 13 years old, bravely asked Roberts to shoot her first and allow the others, the younger children, to go free.

Instead, Roberts chose to shoot all of them. Within minutes, three of the girls lay dead and the other seven lay critically wounded. Two of the girls, sisters, would die the next day. One of the girls, just seven-year-old, Roberts had allegedly shot twenty times.

What was his motivation? Roberts allegedly told the girls, "I'm angry at God for taking my little daughter." The same daughter who had died nine years before, just 20 minutes after being born. Why when God doesn't keep score. Then, as police stormed the building, Roberts, in his final act, turned the gun on himself. In the end, he, too, would lay dead.

Following the tragic shooting of these ten little girls, news reporters from around the world raced to Lancaster County to tell the story of the horrors of the murders of these innocent children.

Five children who would never know what it would be like to be children again. Another five children, whose innocence had been lost in the blink of an eye, were left with the memories of that day.

Parents were left to mourn their children and forever question why. As parents, we never know what our child will become; for these children's parents, they will never get to find out what their children would have been.

In the end, five little girls lay dead. The Amish community had been rocked. For the millions of people who send their children to school every day without even a second thought for their safety, it made them hug their children a little bit tighter than ever before.

News reports questioned how a man, who had walked his very own two children to the school bus stop that very morning, could do such a thing. Did they bury their anger before they even buried their children, as some reporters asked? Instead, something else happened that further shocked the world. Something quite remarkable.

Within hours of the murders, the Amish families paid a visit to the wife of Charles Roberts. Yet, this visit was not to point fingers, or even lay blame. There were no angry words. There weren't any threats or angered promises. The Amish had another agenda. It was one more appropriate.

Instead, the Amish offered Charles Roberts and his family the one thing that millions of people need, but very few ever know how or want to give---forgiveness. Then again, how can anyone model forgiveness when you do not practice it for yourself?

Within days, even with their grief ever present for their own losses, the families and members of the Amish community even attended the funeral of Charles Roberts.

It has been mentioned that there were more Amish present at the funeral of Charles Roberts than there were people who had ever known Roberts personally. How could even that be?

How could the Amish, even in the midst of their grief over their shocking loss, not choose anger and resentment for what happened? How could they have chosen forgiveness? How is that even possible?

As the burials of the children went on, this story also made people question how the Amish people, or anyone, could forgive this man so quickly. How do you forgive someone who has hurt you, or someone you loved?

For many people, who do find forgiveness, that kind of forgiveness, it often comes after months, even years, of grief. Many, many years. For others, it never comes.

They remain trapped by their guilt and challenged by their anger, frustration, and fears of being hurt again. That is why for millions of people, not every prison comes with a set of bars, even though, every one makes mistakes. I may have made a few typos in the pages of this book and if that bothers you, then, this book is not for you.

You see, for the families of the Amish schoolhouse children, this was not just any kind of forgiveness. It could not be. This kind of forgiveness did not come after the shootings; it actually came before this tragedy ever occurred. Yes, before.

For every one who reads this, the idea that you can forgive somebody for a slight before it even occurs may surprise you, or even anger you. At first, even I didn't understand it.

Even then, the reason why some people can forgive so easily will challenge the way that you look at everyone around you, your friends, your family, your children, your spouse, and even, yourself. It did for me.

You see forgiveness, when someone has harmed you mentally, physically or emotionally, is actually not about them. It is about you. In this book, you will come to discover that that kind of forgiveness is actually the greatest gift that you can ever give yourself. It is almost biblical in scale.

Finding true forgiveness is a moment only a few people will truly understand, or even, begin to understand. The problem is few people ever know where to look to find it in the first place. That is, until now. It is the very moment that I have come to know as...

When God Stopped Keeping Score...

...How To Break Free From A Past Filled With Hurt, Guilt, And Anger Through The Power Of Forgiveness.

R.A. Clark, M.Ed.

March Third Imprints
Philadelphia, PA

Table Of Contents

Author's Acknowledgments...

This book is dedicated to my mother, the late Elizabeth Clark, without your love and words of wisdom; I would not be the man that I am. For my sister, Jama (pronounced Jay-muh); thank you for always being there for me.

This book is dedicated to my brother, the late Sherman Lamont Clark, my uncle, Harold Labell and to my grandfather, the late Robert Luckey. Thank you for showing me how to be a man in a world that you did not bring me to.

This book is also dedicated to my sons, Javaun and Saymere. The greatest wish, that any parent can ever have, is for their children to have more than they ever did and to be more than they ever were.

This book is also dedicated to a very wise woman, the late Mary Davis. Your words of wisdom will echo for many years to come. Your presence will be missed; yet, it lives on in your family, especially your daughter, Patricia. Thank you both.

In addition, this book is dedicated to the good friends that I have made along the way, Shereatha Green, who is proof that God truly brings people into your life for a reason.

I would like to give a special thank you to the many people that have helped me so much along the way...Oprah Winfrey once said, "Whenever you meet somebody, never say hello. Ask what are you here to teach me?" Good or bad, somebody will always teach you something, if you are willing to learn.

So here is a special thank you to: My grandmothers, Gertrude Clark and Elnora Felder, Carolina Fulmore, Ethel Fulmore, Gertrude Coursey, Joy Matthews, Kathy Carroll, Melva Mitchell, Roxanne Smith, Sharon Carroll, Patricia Williams, Neil Dawson, Dr. Dora Campbell, Patricia Thomas, Brian Thomas, Latifah Sabreen, Veronica Bashir, Linda Sapp, Jim McNeil, Delores Robeson, Gloria Nhambiu, Louella Henderson, Meredith Riley, Gwendolyn Baggett, Carolyn Jones, Deborah Riley, Kim Webb, Brenee Waters, Alethea Ouderkirk, Odette Harris and Beverly Grazier. For anyone who I have overlooked, I apologize.

Finally, to you the reader, of whom God gives much, much is required. For who, you are, is a gift from God, and what you become, is your gift to God...Stay blessed!

"Forgiveness is letting go of the hope that the past can be any different."
- Oprah Winfrey, Talk Show Host

"To forgive is to set a prisoner free and discover that prisoner was you."
- Lewis B. Smedes, Author

"We read that we ought to forgive our enemies; but we do not read that we ought to forgive our friends."
- Sir Francis Bacon, Author

Keeping Score...

Could you forgive someone who has hurt you or someone you love like the Amish? If you are like millions of people, that answer would be a simple no. You can't. You are too busy keeping score to even consider it.

You are too focused on how they hurt you and how you plan to get back at them to even begin to think about forgiveness. You know, keeping score. Some call it nursing a grudge. Very few people are willing to talk about this kind of resentment. Yet, everybody has felt it at one time or another.

The adult child that feels contempt and anger for something their parents did (abuse) or didn't do (neglect) for them as children. The wives who are very quick to remind their husbands of a slight that the husband may have caused and apologized for years ago.

How many women have come to hate their children as a reminder of a failed relationship? Each day the child, in looks and manner, serves as a constant reminder of what that woman lost and what should have been in that failed relationship.

The father may not love the mother any more. The mother may no longer love the father. They may find themselves always arguing or fighting. Neither one remembering that at some point, that each person was exactly what the other person wanted.

What this anger, resentment, guilt, and pain shows is that, for millions of people, not every prison comes with a set of bars. That is because at some point, no matter who you are, regardless of your race, creed, religion or even gender, everyone has suffered at the hands of another person, whether the person intended to hurt them or not.

The question now is whether this wrong happened two minutes, or twenty years ago, whether the person, who has hurt you, is living or dead, why are you still allowing yourself to suffer because of it?

Why is this pain still being allowed to destroy the very relationships that you may have with your friends, family, God, and even yourself?

You may have tried to seek help for your problem. Yet, somehow, deep down inside, you may still feel something is wrong. Even, then, this pain is still quietly destroying every one of these relationships.

Somebody once asked me, how could this pain destroy anyone's relationship with God? The answer is simple. People tend to blame God because they often question how God can allow them to suffer the way that they have. Do you think God would hurt you on purpose? He wouldn't.

For anybody else, I understand that the other person may have lied. They may have deceived you. They have hurt you. So they deserve to suffer, right? Why should you forgive them? Would you change your mind if I told you that the person that needs to be forgiven the most is you?

Again, no matter who you are, everyone has hurt someone, or has been hurt, by the actions of others. It could have been something as small as harsh words said in frustration to your child that morning or the fight you had with your mother last month.

Everyone, from the person who cut you off in traffic, to even you, yes, you yourself, has hurt you in some way, shape, or form. The issue at hand is not what happened, but how you handled it.

With that said, let me ask you this, who was it for you? Who was the last person that got you so angry or upset? Was it your parents? A so-called friend. A spouse? An ex-lover? On the other hand, was it somebody you do not even know?

For millions of people, the answer is probably you, yes, you. You are often the person that is hurting you the most. What is making all of this so bad is that you do not even realize it.

Wait, I am getting ahead of myself. Let's talk about how. The next time that you get upset or angry about anything, remember the only thing that could ever happen to you is what you will allow.

Bad things happen to even the best of us, but nobody controls how you respond to it. Therefore, when somebody upsets you, you have allowed him or her to upset you.

In essence, you chose to play the victim and that hurts more. You have a reason to be angry, but do you have a right to suffer because of it? Let me say it, again, you have a reason to be angry, but you don't have a right to suffer because of it.

Often, as human beings and people in general, we let the littlest things upset us. Everything from a traffic jam during rush hour to a missed appointment. Anything can upset our day. It does not matter how small.

God forbid your parents did something wrong to you as a child and you have paid for it the rest of your life. Instead of you just forgiving yourself for it, because, you had no way to stop it. Instead, you find yourself blaming your parents. Then, again, blaming your parents is often too easy.

You see what happens, then, is that you often continue to blame your parents as the source of your misery and pain, even as an adult. The problem is they are not responsible for every decision that you have made since then. You are responsible.

Instead, of embracing forgiveness and allowing ourselves to move on, anger, guilt, resentment, hurt and pain, instead, becomes your way of life. Your pain becomes the only thing that you, or any of us, know that is real. You are keeping score.

My aunt, Patricia Davis, always says that "a poor rat only has one hole to crawl into." Before you start thinking that anyone is calling you a poor rat, you should know that she got this expression from her mother, Ms.

Mary Davis. It is an age-old expression that simply means that we do what we're used to.

We are creatures of our habits. When faced with the unfamiliar, we tend to turn to the things that provide us with comfort or simply the things that we know.

Habits, even bad ones, are comforting. It wraps us up in a blanket that will never truly warm us, while eating away at what we know that is true about our lives. It's almost like an addiction. A very bad one. It doesn't have to be that way for you or anyone else.

The truth is that good and bad things are going to happen to everyone, regardless if you see them as good or bad. Some things we simply have no control over. None.

Yet, even then, it is not always, what happens to you that matters; it is how you deal with it that matters the most. One of the best ways is through forgiveness. You should always forgive early and forgive often.

Some people ask, in a world with so much pain, how can you ever truly forgive anyone? Just because forgiveness seems to be beyond us, that does not mean it cannot happen. It does happen and will happen even for you, if you allow it to become a part of your life. Here's how…

Right now, I need you to do something for me. I want you to think about all of the things that you have done wrong in your life that you have asked God to forgive you for.

Then, ask yourself, if God can forgive you for these things, what makes you think that other people aren't good enough to be forgiven by you? Even, then if God can forgive you, why haven't you ever forgiven yourself as well?

You see when you forgive, you are not denying that something happened. You do not excuse the person or pretend that it never happened. The past cannot be changed. The only thing that can be changed is how we see it and respond to it.

You don't remove all the consequences for what happened. You do not overlook anything. You are not condoning the person's behavior, or what the person truly did, and you never should.

You are not giving anyone permission to hurt you again. You can't pretend you weren't hurt. No one is going to suddenly confess that they hurt you. They just won't do it.

True forgiveness must come from your heart, not theirs and you do not need an apology to give it. It is not something that anyone should have to earn. For you to hold on to the resentment, that only increases the damage and prolongs the pain that you are feeling.

If a person has to earn your forgiveness as they do your respect, they wouldn't need it in the first place. Even then, how can you expect something from someone who does not know how to give it?

Forgiveness is about letting go completely and permanently within you. It's not about who is to blame or who is at fault. Laying blame only allows them to take advantage of you all over again. Blaming others continues to give them control over your problems, instead of you finding a solution for them.

Wait, let me slow down, maybe I am moving too fast. Maybe, I need to take a few steps back before you can take a needed step forward. Before we go any further, there is something you really need to know. There is another reason why you can't forgive. The answer is as simple as why you can never love, respect, or trust anyone either...

Settling Scores...

When you think about such tragic events that have occurred in this country from the events of September 11th to the shootings at Columbine and Virginia Tech, it seems very easy to hold on to the pain and anger. We cannot forgive, because we cannot forget.

I know that pain is pain. You can't help what you feel. It is even harder when the person that caused the pain seems to go on with their lives, with or, without punishment or even worst, they are already dead.

I will not disrespect you by expecting you to open your heart to anyone who chose violence as a means to end his or her own suffering. Instead, I am asking you to find the strength so that you never have to apologize for someone else's mistakes.

If no one has ever truly told you about forgiveness, let me be the first. Especially when, right about now, you might be also thinking, why should you have to forgive anyone for anything any way? They are the ones that hurt you.

In your anger, you should know that, you have opened your mouth to express your pain, but closed your eyes to the truth about the situation. It happens to almost everyone.

The truth is there is a very real reason why we find ourselves wanting, and at times, needing to keep score in the first place. It is also the reason why we have this insatiable need to settle scores as well.

Why? It is because we have not found it in us to forgive ourselves in the first place. When someone has hurt us, we cannot forgive ourselves for allowing it to happen in the first place. We tend to think about all of the things we could have said or done.

If only we had paid more attention. If only we had taken a left turn, instead of taking a turn to the right. If only... What if I... I should have... I could have...

You cannot forgive anyone until you find forgiveness for yourself for allowing it to happen. In order to be forgiven, for the things we do wrong, we too must learn to forgive.

The same way you can never love someone until you love yourself first, is the same way, you can never find forgiveness of others unless you find it for yourself.

If you bump into someone, you will say sorry or apologize with a simple "excuse me." If you are late, you will apologize. However, what about for you, have you ever apologized to yourself? Probably not.

I am not saying for you to say sorry, I am talking about you looking in the mirror and truly apologizing to yourself. Probably not. Therefore, how then can you ever apologize to someone else when you are not good enough for even you to apologize to?

Do not let somebody do something wrong to you though. They just have to be punished, they have to be hurt. It is only fair. What they did was not a mistake. They meant to do it. For that alone, they need to be punished.

It also only adds insult to injury when somebody asks you what happened. The minute you say it, they want to tell you about what they would have said or done. They may even try to tell you what you should have said or done. They may want to shake their head disapprovingly at you.

At that moment, you start thinking to yourself what you should have done or what you should have said. You will probably get angry all over again. It happens to all of us.

So, what do you do about it when somebody hurts you again? Do you get mad? Do you get even? They yelled, so you yelled back. They hurt you, so you hurt them right back. The problem is, when someone has done something wrong to you, you are not always paying him or her back for what they did.

In our vengeful state, we tend to make people pay for what someone else did. It is only fair; they probably were only making you apologize because somebody else messed up with them. The cycle never ends unless you are prepared to end it.

You see when we are angry with someone else from our past; it is not always this person that we hold accountable for it. They probably were never punished for their wrongdoing. More than likely, they probably never will be. It is the people, around you, that will suffer. I will get to why soon enough.

So, now that we touched on it, let us talk about the people from your past that already hurt you. Did you cut them off from your life and vow to never see them again? What happens then? How do you then settle that score then? Silence doesn't work. Trust me.

You probably said anything at that moment that you could have thought of that would hurt them in the heat of the moment. Good for you! Right? Wrong. What good would that do, except stoop you to their level? Inflicting more pain will not ease your pain.

On the other hand, you may have found some other ways to make them suffer. Maybe they will never see your children again. I will show you Mom and Dad. Is that your way of getting even with them? You sure fixed them.

All of that happens, even when you know that in your heart, your children do not have anything to do with what happened. You will only hurt your children more in the process because no matter how bad you think your parents are; your children might love them more than you will ever know.

For some grandparents, a grandchild is that grandparent's chance to make things right. Before you ever begin to justify what you did by saying what they did, or said, stop yourself. This is not why we are here. We are not here to point fingers, or lay blame towards anyone, not even ourselves. I have something else planned for you.

Let us get back to the matter at hand. How many times have you heard of the wayward son, or daughter, coming home, guilt ridden, for the funeral of the parent, or loved one, who they never said goodbye to?

It took a tragedy to reunite them and even then, it was too late. Will that be your fate? How "even" are you getting if in the end you are the one that loses? Not once did you stop and think that getting even will stoop you down to their level.

You are just as bad as they are. Two wrongs will never make anything right. It never will. Here you are now so consumed with hatred and anger and in the end; they will go on with their lives. What about you?

Chances are you are the only one holding on to your hatred and anger. Chances are they have moved on with their lives and you have not. You are instead bitter and angry in your attempt to keep score.

Every negative word and action that follows is your way of settling that score. That cheating spouse has remarried someone younger and according to him or her, better than you. Every time you see them, they look so much happier. You are not. You might talk about your ex and their new spouse in a negative way every chance that you get.

God forbid your children ever talk about their stepparent and say anything good about them. Your children are going to like the new stepparent initially, the stepparent is trying to win your ex's heart through your children.

Maybe they are really good to your children. Then again, if circumstances were reversed, what would you be doing? What would you want anyone to say about you?

That is not to say that they, the new spouse, are any better than you are. They might be worst in many ways. You will never know because you do not live in that house. They, your ex, have found someone who is essentially just not you. You really should move on from that kind of drama.

That's because, even in your breakup, did you ever stop and think that maybe any wrong, action or issue, that caused the problem in the first place, was not entirely your fault? Maybe, you are not always the reason for someone else's misery, but in their need to blame somebody for what they did, or didn't do, they blamed you.

Despite you knowing any of this, it is almost, as if, resentment and anger simply feels better for you. The anger that you feel should ensure that the other person suffers for what they did to you. There is a problem with thinking like this. There is a huge problem.

As actress and author Carrie Fischer once said, "Resentment is like drinking poison and waiting for the other person to die." The problem is they never do. The only one left to suffer because of this is you.

What happens if the person who hurt you is long dead and gone? Why are you still harboring these feelings of resentment, hatred, anger, and unease? They are not suffering any more. Why should you?

This is often no different than if the person was arrested, convicted and sentenced for the crime. Why are you a prisoner of your fear that they can hurt you all over again? People can only do what you allow. That fear is the interest on a debt that you do not owe.

Fear is the belief that something wrong can happen and if you expect it, it usually will. On the other side is faith, both are beliefs that something can happen, but with faith, it is for the best. It should always be that way.

Fear says that somebody has hurt you and if you let him or her, he or she will hurt you again. However, with faith, faith says you are aware of what they are capable of and you have faith in yourself never to allow it to happen again. Even if it does, you are able to deal with it because you dealt with it before.

The truth is when you made the decision to hold on to your anger; you also made the choice to allow yourself to suffer because of it. Why? Again, the only thing that can ever happen to you, when it comes to your feelings and responses, is what you allow.

I have a firm belief that changed anyone's ability to hurt me emotionally, mentally or physically. It is as simple as a reminder that "He, who angers you, controls you."

When somebody has the ability to make you upset, they will always have that control. You gave it to them and you didn't even know it.

You could be on your way to the greatest day of your life, but consider what that one thought, the sound of their voice, and sight of a person that you do not like or even, something that reminds you of them, can do.

Hence, the idea that he who angers you controls you. You are just like a telephone; they know how to push your buttons. If they can push your buttons today, they can always push your buttons, today, tomorrow and even a year from now. Just watch.

That is why the forgiveness that you need in your life should always be about you and not them. Forgiveness is defined as "to stop feeling anger and resentment towards a person, or at an action that has caused upset or harm."

Therefore, forgiveness is the greatest gift that you can ever give yourself. You are not giving the person permission to do it again. You will not let them hurt you again.

You are forgiving yourself first, this is the one person who always deserves your forgiveness, and others come second. As with anything, there is a catch to even forgiveness, it's the forgetting part.

Many people will try to tell you to forgive and forget, but you can never forget. For anyone that has ever tried, there is a reason why I am actually glad you failed at trying to forgive and forget. Actually, you should never try...

Forgive And Remember...

There is a story about forgiveness that I once heard, that I don't recall who wrote or even said it. It goes something like this:

Two friends were walking through the desert. They had an argument; and one friend slapped the other in the face.

The one, who was slapped, was hurt, but without saying anything, wrote in the sand: TODAY, MY BEST FRIEND SLAPPED ME IN THE FACE.

They kept on walking until they found an oasis where they decided to take a swim. The friend, who had been slapped, had gotten stuck in the muck and started drowning.

The friend saved him. After he recovered, he wrote on a stone: TODAY, MY BEST FRIEND SAVED MY LIFE.

The friend, who had slapped and saved the other, asked, "After I hurt you, you wrote in sand. Then, you wrote on a stone when I saved you. Why?"

His reply, "When someone hurts us we should write it in sand where winds of forgiveness can erase it away. Do not dwell on it. Let it go. When someone does something good for us, we must engrave it in stone where no wind can ever erase it."

The moral is this: Learn to write your hurts in sand and carve your benefits in stone. It's said it takes a minute to find a special person, an hour to appreciate them, a day to love them and a lifetime to forget them.

Sounds nice, but I am here to tell you that there is a big difference between forgetting and dwelling on the matter. If you dwell on the issue then you are giving the pain permission to haunt you.

In turn, you are giving the pain a chance to resurface and hurt you all over again. In truth, you don't always have to hold on to the pain to hold on the memory.

That's why I have to agree with what John F. Kennedy once said about forgiveness. John F. Kennedy, one of the greatest presidents that ever lived, said, "Forgive your enemies, but never forget their names."

In simple terms, you should know that if knowledge is power, it is always better to know what people are capable of and what they can do. By not dwelling on the slight, you are not giving it the power it needs.

You haven't dismissed it as if it never happened, but you are not giving it the ability to fester like a sore and harm you. That is also not to say you will be free from the pain just yet. There is a reason for any pain.

As we move through this book, in forgiving a slight, you will discover this slight will no longer hold the same power over you. For far too long, when something hurts us, this pain has this uncanny knack for showing up when we least expect it.

By not forgiving the slight, or what caused it, we have already given it the ability to replay those same feelings without our permission. Forgiveness restores your power for when those feelings surface, it will be on your terms how you deal with them.

The pain you felt at the initial offense will no longer have permission to surface without your permission to hurt you all over again. That's why finding forgiveness is the best way to right any wrong. It is not based on anger, or harming anyone. What can you gain by passing on your pain?

Instead, forgiveness is also about prevention and protection. When the pain you feel begins to resurface and it will, it will not reopen old wounds. Second, the person who harmed you no longer has your permission to hurt you ever again.

Had Charles Roberts lived, the Amish would have sought out justice for what he did. I am sure that the legal system would have gladly given it to him, not just for the sake of punishing him. This move would have been also to protect other children that he might have hurt. This might have included his own. Could Charles Roberts hurt his own children? The world may never know.

We still do not know the real reasons why he walked into that schoolhouse in the first place and hurt the children that he did hurt. If we always knew what other people were thinking, or planning to do, this world would be a very different place.

That's why in forgiving but never forgetting a slight, we will always have a warning. With any wrongdoing, for anyone to seek justice should be about doing what needs to be done regardless of what we feel about the situation. Forgiveness works the same way.

If you knew that every time somebody walks past your seat, the person will step on your foot. You will move your foot. Even if the person that almost stepped on your foot isn't the one that originally stepped on your foot.

That is a crucial step in finding forgiveness. You have to acknowledge what happened. Forgetting makes it seem like things never happened. Nothing has gone wrong.

In forgetting a slight, that means not dealing with the reality of the situation. Fantasy may be what you want, but reality is what you need. This is the reality.

That is no different than if you knew somebody was out to hurt you, or someone you love, or was even capable of it, you would move him or her out of harm's way.

Remember this, because this is what is happening with your memories of past events, now is your first chance to stop them from doing harm by changing how you see them. How? By forgiving the very thing that caused them in the first place.

The Amish's ability to forgive Charles Roberts was based on the knowledge that to be forgiven, you must be willing to forgive. That kind of forgiveness will not happen on its own. You have to be willing to work towards it.

There is only one problem with even that. Everyone thinks that they know what forgiveness is, but few people ever get it right. I didn't at first. It is constant practice that brings success at it.

I soon learned that one of the key ingredients to forgiveness has always been self-control. Self-control means knowing that you can do something, like seeking revenge, but deciding you will not.

That is why millions of people pay the cost of refusing to find forgiveness. Even when it is, being offered to you, many people still refuse to accept it. Some just cannot do it, because they cannot forget what happened. When in doubt, forgive what you cannot forget.

If not forgiving is your attempt to keep score, you are making one of the biggest mistakes of your life. Right now, I think I need to show you better than what I can tell you what forgiveness really is…

Understanding Forgiveness...

A young man was getting ready to graduate from college. For months he had admired a beautiful sports car in a dealer's showroom, and knowing his father could well afford it, he told him that was all he wanted.

As Graduation Day approached, the young man awaited signs that his father had purchased the car. Finally, on the morning of his graduation his father called him into his private study.

His father told him how proud he was to have such a fine son, and told him how much he loved him. He handed his son a beautiful wrapped gift box.

Curious, but somewhat disappointed the young man opened the box and found a lovely, leather-bound Bible, with the young man's name embossed in gold.

Angrily, he raised his voice to his father, said, "With all your money, you give me a Bible?", and stormed out of the house, leaving the Bible.

Many years passed and the young man was very successful in life. He had a beautiful home and wonderful family, but realized his father was very old, and thought that perhaps he should go to him. He had not seen him since that graduation day.

Before he could make arrangements, he received a telegram telling him his father had passed away, and willed all of his possessions to his son. He needed to come home immediately and take care of things.

When he arrived at his father's house, sudden sadness and regret filled his heart. He began to search his father's important papers and saw the still new Bible, just as he had left it years ago. With tears, he opened the Bible and began to turn the pages.

His father had carefully underlined a verse, Matthew 7:11, *"And if ye, being evil, know how to give good gifts to your children, how much more shall your Heavenly father which is in heaven, give to those who ask Him?"*

As he read those words, a car key dropped from the back of the Bible. It had a tag with the dealer's name, the same dealer who had the sports car he had desired.

On the tag was the date of his graduation, and the words...Paid In Full. How many times do we miss God's blessings, because they are not packaged as we expected? How many times do we say words that we later regret?

With this kind of regret, you are harboring feelings over what you may have done in the past. You should not have said that. You should not have done that. You were too busy burning bridges.

Right now, whatever you think that you know about forgiveness, let us put it to the side for a moment. It is time somebody finally told you the truth about the lies that millions of people tell themselves, "I forgive you,"" I'm sorry" and "I apologize."

Again, forgiveness is defined as "to stop feeling anger and resentment towards a person or at an action that has caused upset or harm." As Oprah Winfrey once said, "Forgiveness is letting go of the hope that the past can be any different." Most people tend to confuse getting over regret with forgiveness. There is a big difference.

My grandmother used to say you never know whom you will have to ask for a glass of water. That is why it's not always good to burn bridges. The bridge that you may burn today may very well have to be the bridge that will carry you across tomorrow. People often burn these bridges in anger.

I personally love anger. I have learned that in anger, that's when a person's true feelings come out. Their adrenaline is pumping and they say things that they wouldn't have always had the courage to say.

When they do, they never say, "That was a lie." No, they say, "I should not have said that." Even a lie has a hint of the truth. Most of our anger is born out of the biggest problem that we ever have with other people. They are usually not the problem, we are.

The truth is we are selfish at times. We are so focused on what we want people to be and do for us and not who they are or what they truly might want or need. When people do not meet your needs, you become frustrated and angry. They may not even know what your needs are.

Most of the anger that you feel is a product of people not meeting your needs. Think about a baby, when their needs aren't met, what do they do? They throw a fit to express themselves. As even adults, remember, we are all somebody's children.

Think about your parents, as babies, we crave their attention. As children, we seek out their approval. As teens, we might begin to question some of their decisions or their opinions when we make our own decisions.

As adults, we start to act just like them whether we realize that we are doing it or not. I say this because, even our parents may not always know, what our needs are. That's why many of them withstand the worst of our anger and are usually the first people we lash out at in our anger and pain.

Think about the last argument or heated disagreement you had with anyone. Afterwards, you may have realized how consumed by your feelings that you were.

You very rarely will remember what you said or did in the heat of that moment. You always remember the feelings but not the words. Somebody has made you mad, angry, or upset, but about what?

Some time later, we are left wondering why we even had the problem with the person in the first place. That is also the problem with saying words in anger. We never get to write them down and because of that, we very rarely get to live them down.

I am a firm believer that everything happens for a reason. It may not happen the way we want it to, but some times, it needs to be said, or done, so we say it aloud to them.

Even if it is in anger, we get so upset that we did not know what to do but yell and hurt back. Then what? That's why I try to choose my thoughts carefully. Thoughts become words, words become actions.

Like the young man and the bible, sometimes we rush too quickly to judgment. We don't take our time. With anything, that's the lesson to be learned, in order to understand forgiveness, take your time.

Forgiveness should never be a quick fix for the moments when you don't take your time. Anything worth having takes time. What is meant to be is going to be, but it should not be rushed.

You do not know how many times I considered writing this book. Yet, it seemed like each time I put pen to paper, something happened and I put the pen down. It was not the right time. The first copy of the book that I wrote, my computer crashed and I lost everything. Then, I started on the one you are reading. It was not time.

Then, one day the title popped in my head and I knew that this too was something that God meant for me to do. When the time was right it would happen and thankfully, it did.

That is also how I feel about forgiveness. Forgiveness is not a race. It is not something you should enter into lightly. What is meant to be will be for there is a time for everything. Even then, forgiveness is not a new idea. Still, you might have to read this book several times to truly grasp every aspect of it.

The secret to forgiveness has been around for thousands of years. It began with one man who stood accused of crimes, but was completely innocent. He stood trial. He was then ultimately crucified for those crimes. That man's name was Jesus Christ.

Even Jesus, in the midst of all his anguish and hardships, knew forgiveness as well. Jesus said "Father forgive them for they know not what they do."

In those simple words, Jesus shared with the world the greatest secret ever known to humanity and the key to your future happiness. It is called forgiveness.

Whenever you are seeking forgiveness, you should know though that you are never forgiving the person though. You are actually forgiving the slight. Wait, you might be still thinking about the words of Jesus Christ that you didn't read what I just said.

In finding forgiveness for any one, you should never forgive the person that harmed, offended, or even upset you. You should always forgive what they did. You are not forgiving your mother, father, brother, sister, child, or even your spouse ever. You are not even forgiving yourself.

When you are forgiving somebody, even yourself, you are forgiving what was done. You are forgiving the wrong that was done. You are forgiving a person for what they did, not who they are. That is a huge step.

Let me say it again, you never forgive the person, you forgive the action that wronged you. The fact that they did something wrong to you makes them human.

Nobody is perfect. Forgiveness means never allowing them to hurt you again the same way. Forgiveness isn't a sign of your weakness, but a sign of your strength.

By forgiving others, you are putting faith in yourself to be a better person. You have to take the initiative to become better. You are easing the guilt that is deep down inside of you and promoting a healing of your mind, body, and soul.

What makes forgiveness harder is that forgiveness will bring on a sense loss of some thing that you thought you once could not live without--the pain. You are not losing anything at that point. God never takes anything from you.

God is only preparing you for something bigger and better. God is preparing you for something more positive and constructive in your life. There is a reason for everything, even the time and way this book came into your life. Look at things, this way...

If you are like most, and questions why things happen when they do, just know that again, some things happen for a distinct reason. Often we aren't ready to deal with some things. Other times, some things aren't ready for us. Not this time. The time has come for you to embrace forgiveness.

With forgiveness, you are no longer bound by the feelings associated with the past.

Forgiveness helps bring the end to all of the negativity you want to feel, the regrets, the hate, the jealousy and the shame.

You only felt that initial pain to tell you that something is wrong. The problem is that you may have not known at that moment how to deal with it. The good thing is that you have already started to deal with it the minute you picked up this book.

Remember, it's all about forgiveness and you. Before we move on, I think I need to prepare you for something else. You see the scariest part of forgiveness has yet to be revealed to you.

You see forgiveness does not always begin with just saying, "Excuse me," "I'm sorry" or even, "I apologize." It's a bit more complicated than that. We should never keep that lie alive. Please don't.

I feel that it's about time that somebody told you the truth about these lies. The problem is nobody ever just told you these lies, these lies were taught.

You see the sins of the father, as they say, don't simply rest on the head of their children. These lies are actually taught...

The Lies We Tell Ourselves and Others...

Two men, both suffering and ill, are being treated in a hospital room. One of them is allowed to sit up in bed for one hour every afternoon. Fortunately, the bed is on the side of the room with a window, the only one in that room. The other man must lie flat on his back.

Every day, they talked to each other during the long hours. They discuss their wives and family, home, work, their involvement in the military and places they had visited during the holidays.

Every afternoon, when the man, still close to the window, is allowed to sit up near the window, he told the other man about what he sees outside the window to his friend across the room.

During the hour, the other man is so happy and exuberant imagining the things the other man sees. "I see a large garden pond. It is beautiful. Ducks and geese swim beautifully, while children play with toy boats."

"Some couples walk by; hand in hand, in the middle of the garden. All kinds of flowers filled the garden," he continued. "The flowers

49

were in every color of the rainbow. A large old tree decorates the park. Far above the skyline of the city seen there, a beautiful dusk is settling."

The first man told of the situation outside the window with such great detail that the other man felt like he was there. With each day, his spirit becomes stronger and it gives him a greater incentive to live despite his pain.

The next day, the man who sat near the window told about the carnival parade on the road outside. Although the second man cannot hear the parade, he can see through the eyes of the first man that describe all of the beautifully things he sees.

This goes on for days on end. Weeks pass. Then, months pass. One morning, a nurse came and he found the man, who slept near the window, had died quietly in his sleep.

Sadden by the loss of his friend, the second man ask the nurse to be moved to the other side of the room. The nurse was only happy to help the man move. When the move was done, she left the man alone in the room.

Slowly and in pain, this man forced himself to rise. He wanted to see the beauty of the outside world through the window. He was close enough to see it for himself now.

Heart tense, slowly, he raises up to look out the window. He is immediately surprised by what he sees. What? It turns out that window overlooked another wall.

He called to the nurse right away. He asks what happened to the window. He told her the stories that the man, who slept in the bed before him, told him. What happened to the gardens, the parade, the flowers, and the trees? They didn't just up and disappear.

The nurse said, to the man's surprise, that the first man was blind. He could not even see the wall. When the man asked the nurse, why would the other man lie in such a way?

"Maybe he wants to keep your spirit alive," said the nurse...

Why would people lie? The truth is we only do what has been done to us. When a person lies, they think they are doing it for our own good. That is apart of the reason why when things go wrong, we lie to ourselves.

How many times have you said you are okay when you know you really are not? It happens. Lies are easy. It is easier to seek forgiveness than ask for permission in a case like that. Little white lies are okay if you are telling people about you. Right?

How many times have you asked somebody how does something look and he or she tells you that it looked fine? It could be another lie. Why should they truly care, they do not have to wear it. How do you think it looks? You will know it is a lie when during an argument; they bring it up in an insulting way.

Like the blind man, so many people have led you into this false sense of security. I don't believe in lies. Why lie when the truth will do? If we are going talk about forgiveness, let us also talk about what forgiveness truly is.

With forgiveness, if you forgive a person, it is not an end to a bad situation. You will not wake up tomorrow and say everything will be okay. Something bad still happened.

That is like sweeping a broken vase under the rug, the broken pieces still show. That is like when somebody has broken your heart, it still shows. Every last piece of your broken heart will still show.

The next time that you are cut off in traffic, you will not thank the person that cut you off with all five fingers. You won't. Forgiveness actually takes time and practice. Something like you being cut off like that should not take long to forgive. At that moment though, you are not thinking about forgiveness.

Even then, not all of your bad feelings will quietly go away. They will never go away because the pain is a reminder that something bad occurred. That is what pain is supposed to be, a sign that something is wrong.

I would be lying to you, myself, and God, if I told you every negative feeling in your life will just vanish. Things do not go away completely. You can't change that.

There is some thing that you can change. You can change how you perceive them and how ultimately, you react to them. If your problems ever magically disappear, then you would not be human.

The truth is that you should acknowledge how you feel when a problem surfaces. If you don't you will see that the first casualty of negative, or bad, feelings is usually your self-esteem, how you feel about yourself.

People tend to lower or raise their self-esteem to meet the expectations that other people have of them. Millions of people do it every day and they don't even know it. Wait, let me explain.

Let's say, if somebody loves you, you are sitting on cloud nine. You feel like you are on the top of the world. You will feel it. They will feel it. They will show you how they feel.

Now what if they do not like you, or if they do not expect anything of you, chances are you will not expect anything of yourself. The truth is you cannot continue to live your life longing for people to make things right for you, especially when somebody has hurt you.

The person that has hurt you will not always admit guilt. If you ever tried to wait, you might be waiting a long time. What if the person does not even know that they hurt you in the first place? What happens then?

Again, how can you expect something from someone who doesn't know how to give it? It could be love, acceptance, trust, or forgiveness. Think about it.

Some people will not say "sorry." They will not try to make things right. Have you? For everything, you have done wrong, do you always apologize?

If you said you do, are you being honest with yourself? Is that another lie that we tell ourselves, and others, to get though our day? You may try hard to, but, what about the things you do not even know that you did.

Remember, some people apologize just as a way to move on. I am sorry and all is forgiven. Is it? No.

Let me say it in Spanish—no.

Let me say it in English—no.

In Italian—no. French--no.

Again, what if you do not know who did something to wrong you? What if the person has harmed you and then, you found out later on that they are dead and gone? That is why forgiveness becomes that much more of a powerful tool for you.

Forgiveness, again, does not mean you will suddenly forget what happened. You are not excusing the other person for what they did. I am a firm believer that excuses only please the people that use them.

Excuse me. I am sorry. I apologize. Words, like this, are kicked around so much by most people that there is only one true way to be able to tell when it is real, even when you are saying it to yourself. You must be honest.

In the mean time, remember that you should never forget when somebody has wronged you. You will not always think about it, but, in the back of your mind, it is there.

I have found out the hard way that it is okay to not be okay when you truly aren't feeling okay. If you are angry, say that you are angry. If you are upset, say that you are upset. If you are disappointed, say it aloud.

Why lie when the truth will do? Whoever said the truth hurts probably said it because somebody told the truth about them.

Otherwise, the pain, when we have been hurt, is always lying in wait until somebody hurts you again, and then, without forgiveness to protect you, like an open wound, the new hurt only adds salt to the open wound.

Forgetting a slight and not forgiving will set you up for failure that most people do not always recover from. That's because forgiveness is not your excuse to move forward or to help dull the pain.

Forgiveness is your opportunity to move forward. You have to know what needs to be changed by examining what has hurt you.

In a world where it is hard to love, when there is so much to hate, you need to remember that forgiveness is for you, not them. However, before we can even get to that moment let us deal with something I call the "hurting process."

It's something you need to be completely honest about. Nobody can truly begin to heal the pain in his or her life and move forward until the hurting process is over.

What is this "hurting process?" It is the moment when you need to face your fears and decide that now is the time to stop apologizing for other people's mistakes...

The Hurting Process

At this point, you will probably ask is if forgiveness is such a painful process, why even attempt it? The truth is it is not the journey for you to consider but the destination. The destination is to bring an end to the anger, resentment, guilt, and pain. That is what you should consider.

Let me tell you a story...A teacher once told his class to bring a clear plastic bag and a sack of potatoes to class. For each person you refuse to forgive for whatever reason, no matter what that person did, the student should choose a potato and write the person's name.

They also have to write down why they cannot forgive the person, wrap that around the potato, and put it in the bag. Each student was to carry the bag with him or her for the next two weeks.

When the students slept, the bags should lay waiting beside the students' bed. No matter where they went, they should carry this bag. Eventually, the weight of carrying around these potatoes became clear to the students. It was an emotional and spiritual weight.

Suddenly, the students became conscious to not leave the bag just anywhere. Not just because of the words written on the paper wrapped around the potatoes, but the potatoes themselves. The potatoes had started to rot and smell.

The potatoes had started to deteriorate, just as things went from bad to worst because of the resentment that they carried. This was the lesson to be learned.

Remember what I said before, forgiveness is not something you do for other people. It is something you do for yourself. The minute that you see this for yourself begins what I call the "hurting process." It started the moment you opened this book, your mind subconsciously said that you needed help.

It is not a healing process until you acknowledge what happened. For many people, you are often in denial as to what is truly hurting you. Maybe, it is because you are still dealing with it.

Are you in a relationship that is not working? Are you in a job that you hate? Are you estranged from your parents because of something that happened years ago?

Then, you have not found that moment that I mentioned before that the Amish already know. It is the moment when even God stops keeping score. It is the moment of total forgiveness of yourself and others, when you have learned to forgive others and, more importantly, yourself.

Trust me, it does exist, but how can you begin to find forgiveness, if you do not even know that you do not know that you need it in the first place or where to look?

Take a moment to think about this, when you wake up in the morning, what do you see when you look into the mirror? Have you ever truly looked at yourself? No? Then take a minute to do it now. I will wait.

What do you see? I will bet you the price of this book that you never truly see what is truly there. This is the biggest challenge in finding forgiveness for others; you have to see things for yourself first.

When you look in the mirror, you are not seeing you. You are seeing a continuous collage of past and present experiences based on forgotten praises, remembered insults, constant worries, and thoughts about what should be, instead of what is there.

60

Let me say it again. You are seeing a continuous collage of past and present experiences based on forgotten praises, remembered insults, constant worries, and thoughts about what should be, instead of what is there.

Think about the things that you wear repeatedly, just because somebody said that they liked it, or paid you a compliment on it. Somebody liked it on you. Pain works the same way.

Each time someone hurts you, in any way, shape and form, it reminds you of all the past wrongs that have occurred in your life. These are things that you collected, instead of being forgiven and moved on from.

The problem is, as children, from an early age, we are taught to say "sorry," "excuse me," or even how to "apologize." Eventually, when we have been hurt enough by anyone, a person's attempt to apologize becomes "a pile of lies" to us.

We, then, use that collage to put on a brave face to fool the world and protect us from being hurt any further. This brave face, who we want people to see us as, is often based on what other people thought of us.

However, where do all those insults and hurts go? It is called personal baggage. That is where the baggage, like the potatoes, comes in to play. For all the emotions that do not register on our face or roll off our backs, as they say, we collect it into our baggage.

We all have baggage. The difference is whether we have a knapsack, or a matching set of luggage. Each bag contains its own set of issues that we carry into every situation. Not to mention the baggage that people put on us to carry for them.

For example, you do not get along with your father, so you clash with anyone that reminds you of him. It could be anyone from your overbearing boss to your father-in-law that reminds you of him.

Is your boss is always on your case, huh? Just like dad was. Maybe, he does not praise you enough, just like dad. Maybe, it is because he reminds you of your father, so you think he treats you like your father does.

Think about the mother, or father, that constantly tells her child that he, or she, is acting just like their father. The mother, or father, may have never said that when they were together. The minute that the two of them broke up, suddenly things changed.

If there truly is a thin line between love and hate, he or she found it. Instead of being, a reminder of something that once was good, the child is now a reminder of what is not there any more. The same relationship that any memory of, including that child, hurts him or her. Again, at some point, it's what they both wanted.

Think about a "daddy's little girl," she goes out and dates different people searching for true love. She expects every man to treat her just like her daddy. Then, she gets upset when he does not. What did I say about not meeting other people's needs?

Her excuse is always that she just hasn't found the "right guy?" When I hear those kinds of conversations, I want to scream, do you think it might be you, lady?

Wait! I apologize. My mouth is not a prayer book and the words that I speak are not always the gospel. Therefore, I will agree and say she has not found the right person, one who will treat her like Daddy!

Eventually, you will discover that carrying that luggage around just like that sack of potatoes. Not everyone is going to treat you the same way and I know it stinks.

On the other hand, not everyone is out to hurt you. I am a firm believer that there are only two kinds of emotions in this world: love and fear, which caused all of this.

Never in the history of the world has two emotions driven our anger, pain, guilt and resentment, the same way. Not love and hate, love and fear. Nevertheless, I digressed. Let me get back to the issue at hand, the hurting process.

A few pages back, I mentioned something that I do not think you realized. I said what if what happened that started you packing your luggage was not entirely your fault.

You can't change how somebody treated you, but you can choose how it affects the way you treat other people, including yourself. Wait, especially you.

That is the best part of exploring the hurting process, it is learning to accept responsibility for everything that you do and not the things that people blame you for, but aren't truly yours to claim.

Remember that those nagging feelings, about things that went on in your life, are not based on guilt; they exist because you started packing another bag in your matching set of luggage. You allowed yourself to apologize when other people decided to do wrong to you.

For many of us, we apologize for things that were not our fault. We do it for many reasons; maybe you blamed yourself partly for anything that happened.

Maybe, you wanted to restore the peace. Maybe, you felt that it was the only way for you to move on. However, what did it do to you? How do you feel now?

When I was growing up, I started packing my own set of luggage and developing my own baggage. Bear with me, because I am not good with talking about myself. I feel like I am giving testimony in a high stakes legal case.

You see the most baggage that I ever collected surrounded my father. You see, for anybody that has ever known me, I have been through a lot in my lifetime. During the time my father was on drugs, I lost my mother suddenly. I was only 17 years old.

My mother died of what can be summed up as an allergic reaction to an unknown substance. To this day, we still do not know what it is that truly killed her.

She was not on drugs. She was not a heavy drinker. She did not even smoke cigarettes. She simply went into the hospital one day and never came home again.

My grandmother, who became my legal guardian, suffered a stroke only weeks after my mother died. No parent should ever have to bury their child.

This forced me, at only 17 years old to become the legal guardian of my then nine-year-old sister. What about my father, you ask? People often do.

When told the news that my mother passed away, I was told that he said that he would leave me where I was. At the time, I was already in so much pain that I did not even know if that was supposed to hurt.

It did not help that when I was growing up, I never really knew my father. My friends had fathers, but, where was mine? I did not truly even know that he was my father until I was about eight years old.

My father and his inability to be there for me from the beginning, is when I started packing my bags? In truth, he was in prison when I was born. It was never a secret.

My grandmother said, when he was released he came to see my mother. She told him that I was born and he said, "I don't know if he's mine but I like the little guy." Interesting.

Growing up, if he walked past me in the street, I would not even know who he was. Even when I was around him, he remained at a distance. At my grandmother's house, my cousins used to call him Uncle Charles and I honestly thought that that was his name.

With my father as my guide, I never knew what it was like to be a father, until the day, I became a father. What was I supposed to do? I trusted in God.

Whenever something does not happen, the way I want it to, I soon learned either I wasn't ready for it or it wasn't meant to be for me.

God had something better for me. That is where patience becomes the key. Good things truly come to those that wait. For me, it was the words of my mother.

As the issues with my father began, back then, to surface, my mother said something that began my first lesson in forgiveness ever. She ended the hurting process for me and started me down the path to happiness.

With these two simple sentences, my mother changed how I looked at my father and in turn, how I looked at the world. It stopped me from ever hating anyone. It taught me how to forgive early and forgive often.

To this day, it's because of what my mother said that I truly am able to still treat people right, even in the face of them doing something wrong to me. The temptation to hate them can be strong at times, but I have my mother to thank for me to not give in to that temptation.

It brought me one step closer to the moment when even God stopped keeping score. It changed my life; maybe it can do the same for you. I am smiling right now, because I know you are wondering, what did she say? She said...

The Healing Process....

Are you still with me? Good. Good things come to those who wait. So where were we? There I was starting to become consumed by anger for a father that treated his children like an absentee landlord.

As his children, we were like neglected properties. If we started to show value then we were reappraised. He wanted the credit. He just never put in any work with us.

Waiting in the wings, there was my mother. They say that a mother knows. We often get angry that our mothers can tell us what we are going to do before we do it, but the truth is who else knew us before we knew ourselves? She carried you for nine months. A mother knows, trust me.

So again, there was my mother. My mother recognized my feelings about my father early on and instead of allowing me to play the victim for what my father did not do, she told me what I should do to ensure I never will. She said never hate him.

My mother said I had a right to dislike the things that he did, but that I should never hate him. That is what I did. That was my first and most powerful lesson ever, in forgiveness, that I ever learned. It changed my life.

You should not hate the person, yet, you have a right to dislike the things that they do. Oprah Winfrey even once said, "You can not hate anyone without hating yourself first. It's where you practice hatred first." It is in knowing this that you can forgive them.

What my mother said only made me stronger for when the time came for me to reach out to my father. I told him that it did not cost any thing to be my father. With my own sons, I learned that a walk means more to them than any gifts that I could give them. All I used to want was his time.

After all of that, you may still wonder, did this make my father come running back into my life, with me there to welcome him warmly? The answer is no. He never did anything.

To this day, my father has never been my father. Do I hate him? The answer is no. Honestly, I would have to know him and not of him first. You should also know that my father was severely addicted to drugs for the better part of my childhood.

I say that not as my excuse for him, but that was often his excuse for what he did and did not do for me. If he didn't want anyone to know, then he shouldn't have done them. That is apart of the reason I never used drugs. I now have my own children to consider, as well.

I soon learned that the sins of my father do not rest on my head. So now, when I look in the mirror, I do not see the product of my father's mistakes, but the father to my own children. That is it. Nothing less.

Even, then I do not unpack an issue every time something happens with one of my sons, but look at things that need to be done to ensure their upbringing.

With my sons, I am going to make mistakes, a lot of them, but the only way that I can make a mistake is by actually making an effort. In that one moment, I have become a better man than my father has ever been.

I say that not disrespect him or undermine him. I say it because it is apart of being honest about things. Being honest means that I am being honest about everything. Again, why lie when the truth will do?

Fantasy is often what people want, but reality is often what they need. I retired from the fantasy and the lies. How can you apologize if, within you, all you know is "a pile of lies?" You know the lies that we tell ourselves and others to make our day a little better.

Forgiveness requires honesty. The minute you are not being honest with yourself, everything you say is a lie. If you can lie to yourself, you can lie to me and even God.

I know what you are thinking; did I forgive my father for what he did and did not do as a father? Did I forgive him for putting his addiction before me and his other children? At one point, his addiction had gotten so bad. He ended up in jail.

I found out and I went to court. I was only 18 years old then, a month shy of turning 19 years old. I told the courts that my father needed help. He was on drugs and he needed help. I was over 18.

As his son, if the courts didn't do anything to stop him, I would be ready to do whatever I could to help him. Even if it meant signing him into a drug rehabilitation center, I was ready to do whatever it took, to not lose my dad, so soon after I lost my mother. I wasn't ready for that. Then again, who would ever be ready?

Then, something else happened when my father was locked up. I sat down and wrote him a letter that he carried around with him for some time even after he was released that expressed everything I was feeling.

Writing that letter, I can honestly say felt good. It was actually apart of what my mother said to do. I didn't hate him, but I had a right to dislike the things that he did.

It wasn't about what he did, but how I responded to it. I couldn't control what he did or didn't do. Yet, I could control the level that I allowed it to affect me.

Therefore, the answer is yes, I did forgive my father. I had to. It goes back to what I said about your forgiveness not being dependent on the actions of another person.

I acknowledged that there was a problem. I accepted that I could not change what he did or did not do. Then, I apologized to myself for allowing myself to go through it. The question that I have always wondered is does he forgive himself? The answer shouldn't have surprised me…

The Price Tag Of Your Fears....

I used to ask myself, did my father ever forgive himself for what he didn't do when it came to being a father? I honestly don't know. What I do know is, if he did, he would have reached out to me a long time ago, as I tried to do with him.

Don't get me wrong, I had a good life. Despite what my father did and did not do. Believe me I did, I say that not to try to convince you or myself.

I say that because when my father does something, I think about what my mother taught me when she said I should never hate him but I had a right to dislike the things he did. That is it.

This was a big moment for me, because it led to the moment in which I actually thanked him for what he did not do. It was when I was graduating from a two-year college. I graduated with honors and was on my way to a four-year school by the grace of God.

It was rainy day in May; my grandmothers were both there, two strong women who along with my mother, father, and God, I owe my life to. They had met for the first time.

Then, out of nowhere, my father appeared. He looked at me and I reached out my hand and shook his hand. Then, I walked away.

There was no need to mention that just a short time before, I had gone to court and said what I said. There was no mention of the letter. At that moment, he just wanted to play the role of the proud father and I let him.

My aunt, one of my father's sisters, later asked me why I treated my father like that at my graduation. My grandmother jumped to my defense and said how I shook my father's hand. I asked my aunt what more could I do? There was a reason that I did even that.

You see I didn't shake his hand for coming out in the rain. I didn't even shake his hand for giving me life, though I am grateful. He was good enough to bring me into the world; he just was not strong enough to see me through it.

I had learned that we come through our parents but we come from God. I came to realize that my life turned out just fine without my father. You see I was actually thanking him for walking away, because I do not know what I would have become if he stayed.

For every time I thought that I needed him to depend on, I learned to depend on myself. That is one of the greatest stories that people can ever tell you. People go through so much to try to keep a person in their lives that do not want to stay. Why? What for?

I learned that you could not make a person stay somewhere that they do not want to be. I was not going to try to change my father. I have already learned that the only time that you can change anyone is when he, or she, is a baby. That is it.

Again, your happiness is not dependent on the actions of other people. I could not hold my breath waiting for him to make a move. I learned to take deep breaths without him.

This book is not all about me though. This book is about you. By sharing my story, I wanted to show you how to begin to understand your own story and some of the pain that might result from coming to terms with it. You are certainly not alone.

When it came to my father, I am honest enough to tell you that his absence made me not want to be a father at all, initially. Frankly, I did not know what having a father or being a father meant. That is the thing about resentment. It tends to blind you to everything that goes on around you. In all the time that I used to dwell on what my father was not, I never considered what a father a man like my grandfather, the late Robert Luckey was.

I soon learned that the fact that my father's actions had no bearing on my ability to be a father and actually be a good one. My grandfather taught my brother and I that much. It showed in how my brother treated and loved his daughter.

God showed me better than he could tell me again when I was 16, when my aunt married a man named Harold. My Uncle Harold became the father that a child only dreams of having in their life. To this day, I treat my own sons the way he and my grandfather treated me. They deserve nothing less.

It's because of him that I do believe that everyone that enters you life is there to answer a silent prayer that you asked God for in your life. That is why when you meet someone, you should never say hello, but instead ask, what are you here to teach me.

Good or bad, everybody has a chance to teach you something. It is just whether or not you are prepared to listen. You cannot do that when you are carrying around the seeds of your anger. Resentment, hatred, and anger, like that, carries a huge price tag.

Hatred, like that, has a tendency to take on larger than life quality. Nevertheless, that resentment that you feel is a state of mind. I mentioned that there are only two kinds of feelings in this world and that is love and fear. Love and fear.

As children, we learn what love is. The love that we received, as a child, did not come with any price tag. We do not ask for it. It is given. The opposite of love is not really hatred. It is fear. Fear is the basis for all of the evil that people could ever do in your life. Every single thing.

Stop and think about something that you do every day such as locking your front door. Why do you do it? The truth is you are afraid that someone will take something that belongs to you or harm you.

When somebody loves you, you would not think twice of "locking your front door?" You have an open door policy. With love, you actually let down your guard.

When you carry around resentment and anger, that resentment and anger is a product of your fear that someone will hurt you again. That fear comes from the thought that someone will be happy after making your life miserable.

That baggage that you carry around like that sack of potatoes is a manifestation of your fears. Let's go back for a minute to that boss that is always on your case, you are afraid now that they will start thinking like your parents did.

He, or she, thinks you are not good enough. Your self-esteem drops to meet his or her expectations. You are now susceptible to your fears. You are afraid you will lose your job. That is a whole other set of fears by themselves. If you really want to go there, let us talk about your parents for a minute.

You depended on your parents for your sense of well being. What they said could make or break you, even to this day, for many people. My mother used to tell me all of the time that a teacher has "theirs" so you had better get yours. I had teachers that I never liked, so here my mother was telling me to be just like them. It was a good thing.

I soon learned that she really meant that they had a good education. She wanted me to know that college was not an option. It was a destination. Four college degrees later, I think that she was right.

With my mother, she made me go to school every day. Her rule was that you did not have to go to school, but you had to leave her house. Therefore, I went every day.

For some parents, if they were made to feel, in their growing up, that they would not amount to anything, what are the odds that they would feel the same way about their children? It's more than likely.

For my mother, it was not a second thought that I would get a quality education. Instead, it was the issue of if I believe in it too. That is another key element when it comes to forgiveness. Do you believe in it too? That is the key to the hurting process, for you to understand the source of your pain.

Far too often, we are so consumed, by our fear of bad things happening again, to truly look at what happened that caused this pain in the first place. Something bad happens and often the person says that they don't want to talk about it.

When we do speak up, we tend to become so angry that we often try to make other people pay for somebody else's mistakes like our spouse, our children, our friends or even through, abuse of drugs, alcohol or denial, ourselves.

That's why I need you to do something for me. Not, want; I need you to do this for me. God tends to give you what you need and not what you want. When we want something, people have options of giving it to us. When we need something, it takes on a different urgency in our lives.

Right now, I need for you to take a moment and think about your fears, what angers you, and what issues that you may have. If done right, you will come to understand what roles these issues will continue to have in your life.

Trying to forget it happened is denial. It is like trapping a baby moth in closet. Eventually, it will eat away at whatever there is until a larger problem exists. So, before you move on, take a moment to think about the problems in your life that you may have.

It could be your fear of commitment, why you never seem to have enough of anything from love to money, or when you truly began to hate your job. These problems could have happened twenty years ago or twenty minutes. You need to know why.

The main goal is to understand how they are still affecting you now, enabling you to decide what you intend to do about them. Ask yourself, who caused them? You really do need to be honest about this one. Who was it? Was it you? A family member? Was it your spouse or mate? It may help at this point to make a list.

When did it start? Think back to your earliest memories of what happened. What happened? Try to remember each detail no matter how painful it may be. You cannot know what ails you until you find the point that failed you.

How did this situation make you feel? Did it make you angry? Did it make you sad? Were you disappointed? More importantly, does it still make you feel that way? If it still does, you have only begun to scratch the surface of a serious problem.

When this pain surfaces, remember to not only acknowledge it, but accept responsibility for it. If you cast it aside like it is somebody else's problem, you will never truly begin to deal with it. Remember, forgiveness takes honesty from you.

This is the point where you need to acknowledge your feelings. What do you truly want to do with this pain? Do you want to hold on to it or let it go? Don't be afraid to write these feelings down. If you need to, call somebody that you know and talk it out.

This book is bound to help some feelings that you tried to bury to resurface and somebody to talk to will be the key to moving on. You should never be afraid to seek the help of a certified and trained psychologist or counselor.

For some of us, we may need a quiet place to reflect. For others, we have a deep need to work through it. You know the type, they have something on their mind, and they clean, or even, bake. I have seen it all.

Nobody can tell you how to work through your emotions, as long as it is the right way, a non-violent way, to do so. No one.

It's also key to remember the places that you were when these emotions were brought on. This is a key element to think about because every time you are in that place or something reminds you of it, the pain you felt can, or will resurface. Don't be afraid of what you feel.

If you were in your parent's home, these pains will surface whenever anything connected your childhood home appears. It could be as simple as a conversation about your parents between you and a sibling. It could be a photo from your parents.

Why did it happen? For most people the answer to this is that they do not know. This will play a major part in your life later on whether you are seeking forgiveness or providing it. How do you fell about it?

What feelings did you have about this event? What feelings do you still have about this event? Take your time. Do this for every issue you feel that you need to resolve. It is not a race. Take your time. When you are ready, we are going to discuss the real "who" in all of this and what it really means for you.

In case you didn't know, there are actually three people that can ever hurt you the most, the first, you live with them, every day. Who are these mean and evil people in your life capable of doing so much damage? The answer is quite simple; one of them is you...

Family and Forgiveness...

There once was a woman who had gone through a bitter divorce. After the divorce, her teenage daughter became increasingly rebellious, as teenagers sometimes are.

It culminated late one night when the police called to tell her that she had to come to the police station to pick up her daughter, who was arrested for drunk driving. They did not speak until the next afternoon.

Mom broke the tension by giving her daughter a small gift-wrapped box. Her daughter nonchalantly opened it and found a small piece of a rock. She rolled her eyes and said, "Cute Mom, what's this for?"

"Here's the card," Mom said. Her daughter took the card out of the envelope and read it. Tears started to trickle down her cheeks. She got up and gave her mom a big hug as the card fell to the floor.

On the card were these words: "This rock is more than 200 million years old. That is how long it will take before I give up on you."

It has been said that only three people can ever truly love you like this. Through the good times and the bad, they will be there for you. Who are these people? Your friends, your family, and yourself. They are like a good long distance calling plan; these are also the three people in the world that can ever hurt you as badly.

Everything that we truly learn growing up begins with our families. I am a firm believer that the sins of the father (and mother, for that matter) do not rest on the heads of their children. They are taught. That's why nobody can ever hurt us, or love us, like family.

You might say that some times, strangers do hurt us. However, even with a stranger, they can hurt us, but we can get over it faster than when it is someone that we know.

Why is that? With friends and family, they already know us. They know what makes us happy. They know what makes us sad. They know what can hurt us. We told them all of it.

Think about it. What are the things about you that only your friends and your family know? These are the things that people can use to hurt you. They will do it some times.

I honestly believe that friends honestly come and go. With friends, I tend to subscribe to the reason, season, and lifetime idea. It simply means that every friend in your life is there for a reason, season or lifetime. Some people will show up when you need them. Others are there for a certain time period and a purpose. Then, they move on.

While others, they are there for the long haul, like family. With family, you sure cannot pick them. Let us face it, not everybody comes from the perfect home life. Many of us grew up with the feelings of not being good enough.

You will see this in the overachievers. These are also the people that go all out to impress the people that are around them. That is the only way they earned the love of their parents, they had to go above and beyond.

Then, you have the people that set out to destroy every relationship that they ever have. Have you ever known anyone who jumps from relationship to relationship? That is them. That's what they do.

They never learned how to be alone or loved. They are always searching for true love and affection when they do not even know how to love themselves. I look at people who have been married more than twice as that kind of person. It's often sad, but true.

On the other hand, there are women who always complain that they cannot find a good man to develop a serious relationship with. They never once consider that it might be them. They are often so afraid of being hurt and will not allow themselves to be loved.

The one person that I have never liked was the "controller." I once had a supervisor who took her job far too serious. She is very angry. She is very demanding. She asks more of other people than she asks of herself. Everyone around her felt it, but her.

She once told me you do not write your boss a memo. I laughed at her and said, "I work for the Lord, this is a side job." Feeling flustered, she told me to go back to doing what I was doing, and I did.

The controllers need to be in control. They may have been born out of the chaos that has existed in their lives as children or adults. In her case, there were allegedly marital problems at home.

With a person like they, they feel a need to control what is going on around them to feel safe. This is another habit that is based on fear. They do not know any other way.

The sad part is during another general conversation, long after I had left that position, she brought up the fact that she thought that I did not like her. The truth is I never gave my feelings about her a second thought. If anything, I felt sorry for her.

I saw her controlling behavior as a way to mask her fear of rejection and that is what I did not like. I did not have to be her, so I did not know what she was going through. That is one of my policies, when bad things go wrong, I do not go with them.

Again, many of the issues that we face are a product of our upbringings. As children, we depend on our family for the emotional support and guidance that will see us through a world that we never asked to come to.

Yet, when our parents did not receive that in their own lives, we often become the "victims," as I said, of our upbringing. The controlling personality is often a product of a dysfunctional household.

A person who is abused as child, tend to become an abuser because that is what they have been taught. On the other hand, they just may want to hurt others before others hurt them. It is not always physical abuse; it might be emotional or mental.

With that in mind, I want you to stop and think about the last person that truly made you angry. Was it your daughter? Your son? Your spouse? You mom? Your co-worker who is also a friend? What did they do? Do you feel tense, just at the thought of them?

Does your stomach still do back flips, in the wrong directions, because of something that they said? That person has some control over you. He who angers you controls you.

Sure, you can lie to me and anyone else and say they do not, but they do not even have to be around you to still upset you. If they can make you angry now, they will always have that control over you.

How many thousands of kids go to school angry because of something that happened at home that morning? Think about the co-worker or boss who comes in angry at the world because of their home life.

God forbid something should happen to them, that family member, along the way and you will blame yourself for the rest of your life because things ended on such a bad note.

Speaking of parents, think about how you feel every time you go home to your parents' house. You might feel the same way that you felt as a child. You know the feeling.

You get that feeling that causes you to remember what happened when you were there. Suddenly, you are a child all over again and you act accordingly.

Everything that your parents, or siblings, say will trigger those childhood emotions. Before you get upset, remember you are not hurting anyone with your anger, but yourself. So do not even go there. Do not point fingers.

The pain that you are feeling is a sign that something is wrong. In order for you to move forward, you must first understand what is wrong in the first place, deal with these issues and ensure that they can never hurt you again. That is the only way you can ever find peace of mind.

The feeling of having peace of mind will not create itself. You have to create it and when you see that you enjoy this peace of mind, you will begin to limit the bad feelings.

First, there is something very important that you have to understand about yourself. You are not a victim of your upbringing. You are not. You are no longer dependant on your parents for your well-being. You are not.

When you walk back into your parents' house and you get that feeling of fight (anger, hostility, or resentment) or flight (wanting to leave or avoiding the issue). Remember its okay for you to walk away, for now.

Why would you allow yourself to be subjected to the whims of the mother who do not feel you are good enough? She always wants to compare what you are doing with your children to your brothers and sisters. Hello, they are your children! That's not fair!

I remember growing up when somebody used to tell me, when I did not do what they asked me to do or give them what they asked, that I did not act like their child. I had to tell the person I am not their child.

God forbid you have to put up with that overbearing mother-in-law, who feels that you were never good enough for their child anyway. We all know people like that.

Now every holiday, she sweeps through your home like the Duchess of York and pronounce judgment over your home life. Stop that! It is your house.

It is okay for you to stand up for yourself. Do not play the nice nasty role though. One of my friends, named Latifah Sabreen, a great lady to know, taught me that.

It is when people say the nastiest things in the nicest way at every opportunity. Yet, you should say what you feel.

Remember acknowledging your feelings may be the best way to stopping them from controlling you. Your fear of speaking up may be hindering your attempts to move on.

If your spouse has an issue with it, maybe it's because they may have watched their parents go through the same thing but felt powerless to change it. Now is your time to do just that. Speak up and do it often.

People actually value your silence. They will look at it as consent to continue doing what they have been doing. Well, you didn't say anything. So, I figured it was okay to do it.

If you do not do it for just your peace of mind, do it for your health. Holidays tend to be the most stressful times of the year. Why would you allow that to happen in your home?

They say you can never go home ago. The truth is you can go home again. That place is your home. Who ever do not like the rules of your home, well, they can always go home.

My mother once told me that whenever I go anywhere that I was always supposed to be on my best behavior. She said when you are in someone else's home that you were there on "borrowed time." Your home should always be a place of peace and the minute it is not, you should question why.

If anything, as an adult, when coming from a painful past, use it as a gauge to decide what you do not want for yourself and your children. A painful past should not be a way of life for you now. My father was never there for me, I am an active, dedicated father.

With that said, let us take a minute to talk about your friends. Turn on any talk show and you will see, just like the snake at the end of a tree, there are times when that trusted friend is an enemy that you just cannot see and for good reason...

Friends and Acquaintances...

A little girl who was late coming home for supper. Her mother made the expected irate parent's demand to know where she had been. The little girl replied that she had stopped to help Janie, whose bicycle was broken in a fall.

"But, you do not know anything about fixing bicycles," her mother responded. "I know that," the girl said. "I just stopped to help her cry." Safe to say, the mother agreed.

Not many of us know anything about fixing bicycles, either. In addition, when our friends have fallen and broken, not their bicycles but their lives, none of us knows how to fix that either. We aren't God, or even Jesus Christ.

We simply cannot "fix" someone else's life, even though that is what we would like most to do. However, like the little girl, we can stop to help them cry. That is the best we can do. That is a lot! That is a good friend.

There is a difference between being an acquaintance and being a friend. However, few people ever know what it is like to be a friend. You cannot pick your family, but you can pick your friends. Some come for a reason, season, or a lifetime. These are the like-minded people that you share your sense of the world with. They are easy to talk to, and in turn, you share some of your greatest fears and secrets with them.

Again, as with family, they are also the ones that can hurt you because you have a tendency to give them the ammunition. When we are hurt by the actions of our family, we turn to our friends. However, what happens when these friends hurt us too?

The reason why our friends can hurt us is that they are often substitutes for our family. We expect them to offer that same kind of love and devotion. We never expect them to hurt us just as badly. At times, they do, and they will. What happens then?

These are the people that we can share our misfortunes and misdeeds with. They know our limitations. They share our sense of the world. The problem is, like family, we have a tendency to see ourselves through their eyes. We value their opinions.

Think about that the next time you go shopping with a friend and you ask their opinion. If they are good friends, they will give you their opinion. Yet, ask yourself, do you base your decision on what they said or what you truly feel?

I know it sounds harsh, but not everybody is your friend. You may want them to be, but they are not. I try to have more fingers on one hand than I have friends. Every one of these people has already passed what I call the dollar bill test.

If you ever want to know if somebody is your friend, do something as simple as ask them for a dollar. A dollar? A dollar.

When I was in high school, one of my friends named William Williams asked me for a dollar. I gave him the dollar without question. He pulled out a pocket full of money and gave me the dollar back.

William said he did not need it. I asked him why he even asked me for the dollar. He said to see if he could trust me. I was confused. He said people put more value on a dollar than they do on friendship.

Therefore, if you ever ask somebody for a dollar and they give you it unconditionally, that is somebody you can trust. If they ask when they will get it back, or why you need it, then that is somebody you cannot trust.

97

Imagine if you had to go to that person in an emergency and ask them for a favor. Your child got sick at school and you need a ride. The minute they start asking questions is precious time that is wasted that you will never be able to get back.

I'll be the first to tell you that you are not going to like everybody. Some people are just not born to like everybody. When it comes to inviting a person into my home, the invitation alone is a lot to ask of me. My home is my sanctuary.

I do not even want to break bread with anybody unless I truly know them like that. Sharing a meal is sacred to me. That is not to say that I am not open to meeting new people, but as my mother once said, "not everyone is your cup of tea no matter how much sugar you add to it."

If you limit your circle to true friends, you also limit the people that can hurt you. Believe me, there is a difference between a friend and an acquaintance. That is not say an acquaintance cannot become a friend.

Right now, I need you to do something else for me. I need you to stop, and think for a second, if your friends and family can hurt you, think about what an acquaintance can do. They do not really care if you are hurt or not. They have no stake in you. So take a moment to learn the difference between your friends and acquaintances. You will see how love and fear helps you tell the difference.

True friends are the people you feel safe around because you know that they care about you. A friend will call just to see how you are doing, because a friend does not need an excuse. How many people do you talk to in a day? How many of them say hello as a precursor to ask you to do something?

A friend will tell you the truth, the first time, and you do the same. That is what you love about them, but you fear that a stranger will not do. Why should they? They do not know you or care enough about you to.

You know that if you have a problem, friends are there to listen. An acquaintance will say can I call you back and probably never will. Friends are the people who will not laugh at you or hurt you, and if they do hurt you, they try hard to make it up to you.

They are the people that you love, regardless of whether you realize it or not. They are the people that when you hug them, you do not think about how long to hug, or who is going to be the first one to let go. No fear of rejection there. None.

Friends are the people who stop you from making mistakes and help you when you do. Love. They are the people whose hand you can hold, or you can hug or give them a kiss and not have it be awkward because they understand the things that you do and they love you for them no matter what. Love.

They stick with you and stand by you. They hold your hand. They watch you live and you watch them live and you learn from them. Your life is not the same without them. Love.

The bottom line is that friends are people that you know. Associates and acquaintances are people that you only know of and probably not very well. However, now I have a problem. What if it is not your friends and family that is the problem?

What if the problem is really you? Remember when I said there are three people that can ever hurt you, a friend, a family member, and yourself. Let us talk about the one person that tends to hurt you the most---you...

When The Problem Is You...

Here's a question: If two people are in a boat. Their names are Dan and Repeat. If Dan jumped out who was left? Repeat?

If two people are in a boat. Their names are Dan and Repeat. If Dan jumped out who was left? Repeat?

If two people are in a boat. Their names are Dan and Repeat. If Dan jumped out who was left? Repeat?

When did you get it? Every time you say Repeat, the person telling the joke would then repeat themselves. It is a silly joke. It is also an easy way to tell you a secret about yourself. This is a big one. Still with me?

Eventually, this is the same thing that happens with an apology and the things people do to get to a point where they have to apologize for their actions.

You do something wrong and you apologize. People do something wrong to you and they apologize. Eventually, you have start packing that bag as you remember everything they did to you before.

You might be on guard now, because the person who you thought loved you now has you living in fear. It might not be anything as severe as harming you physically, it could be a lie that they told. Nevertheless, you are still afraid. Very afraid.

Remember, the baggage you carry around is based on fear. Think about somebody who is a pack rat. They collect everything. They will not throw away anything because they fear that they will need it later on.

It is the same thing. You are remembering everything and holding on to it as proof as to why you will need to be angry or hurt later on. You are keeping score for that moment when you might do something wrong and have to say well you did this, this and that.

You are afraid you will not have anything to say when somebody accuses you of doing something to them. Eventually, when you get angry enough, that sense of wronged turns into anger and you will want to get revenge. Even if it is just by pointing out what the other person did. Will it be worth it though?

What if the person who has been doing wrong is you? You say "I am sorry." How many times have you heard that lie yourself? Maybe, that is why people use it so easily.

Somebody was late in meeting you, sorry. They forgot something you said or asked them to do, sorry. Nevertheless, are they really sorry? As the song goes, sorry seems to be the hardest word. It's actually not.

You have to understand these things about people and more specifically, you, in general. How can you begin to deal with other people if you do not know how to deal with yourself first? Even then, we need to be honest.

I asked some time ago, why should we forgive anyway? Especially when, we are not the ones who did us wrong. We can't. Why? Resentment actually feels better to us.

It is easier to hate somebody than to love them because trying to love someone after they have done us wrong brings on that fear that they will hurt us again. Right?

Well, misery loves company too. When things happen, we would rather complain about it than just to move on. That must be why they say when we do not like something, we are more like to tell at least three people than just one. Think about that for a minute.

Not forgiving a person is not always an easy thing to do. People will not always forgive you so why should you forgive them. The bigger the wrong the harder it will be to forgive anyone. Even then, some things are just unforgivable to some people.

What if I told you that you are doing more harm than good? The reason we should always find forgiveness is that if we continue to hold it in, we find ourselves suffering all over again.

Each time we are hurt for no matter what reason, we revisit those feelings. It resides with us, with that baggage that we carry into every situation until we learn to let it go.

That is not to say we are going to be completely healed again, but when we forgive, the power that we give to the person that has hurt us is lessened.

By learning to deal with what ails you, you can determine what you do not want any more from the people who have failed you.

There will be no more fears that this person can hurt us again that way. We no longer accept that we are powerless to stop the bad things that can happen.

I want you to take a moment and recognize your feelings. Ask yourself why you are feeling guilty about what somebody else has done. Just because they said sorry does not mean that you have forgiven them. If you did, you would not still be suffering.

Why do you blame yourself, especially when what happened may not be entirely your fault? Is it because they blamed you? Is it because you felt at fault? On the other hand, did they make you feel that way as a way to ease their guilt? Did they or did you?

Some people will try to put you down to make them selves feel better. They cannot function unless they feel like they have won something. They have not won anything.

The truth is, as an adult, they cannot do anything to you that you will not allow. That is why some times it is better to let people think they have their victory if it means you will keep your peace of mind.

Remember when I said your happiness is not dependent on the actions of others, I meant it. If someone has led you to believe it is, then, they are wrong. It never was.

You are wrong; it is a losing battle. If you feel like you have to right something that has been wronged in your life, you are going to suffer. Let go and let God deal with it for you.

Let me be the first to tell you, that the minute you think that you always have to fight against this kind of abuse and that is what it is, abuse. Emotional abuse to be exact.

You will always live in this constant state of fear. You will fear people rejecting you. You will always fear making mistakes. If you did not make mistakes, how will you ever learn?

You will then become overwhelmed with feelings of not being good enough. Depression is often said to be anger that you turn inward. You will blame yourself.

Remember the casualty for living based on someone else's feelings about you is always your self-esteem. You are still angry. Soothing these hurts with anger, alcohol, drugs, or even the silence that eats away inside of you. That's never a good thing.

You then tend to become more cynical, more hostile. The truth is you should not be affected by anyone's mistakes but your own.

Even then, your mistakes should have been learning opportunities for you to grow.

You must also learn not to point fingers. That is a part of holding on to resentment. Every time that you point a finger, you actually get three pointed back at you. Try it with your hand.

This is the reason why what you wish on others tend to come back on you threefold. The other person gets to go on with their life and more often than not, they do not care that you are angry or upset.

So, what can you do about it? Do you continue to suffer? Do you continue to play the victim? Do you continue to punish yourself long after they have stopped?

Before you even start to think about forgiving, the people that have harmed you in your life, there is something else that we need to talk about. Something that I think is very important to you, or it soon will be.

We need to discuss the one person that you should always forgive no matter what, even when your heart tells you not to—that person is you. I think it's time that we talk about why that is to begin with…

The Gift That You Give Yourself...

A son and his father were walking in the mountains. Suddenly, his son falls, hurts himself, and screams: "AAAhhhh!!!"

To his surprise, hears the voice repeating, somewhere in the mountain: "AAAhhhh!!!"

Curious, he yells: "Who are you?" He receives the answer: "Who are you?"

Angered at the response, he screams: "Coward!" He receives the answer: "Coward!"

He looks to his father and asks: "What's going on?" The father smiles and says: "My son, pay attention."

Then he screams to the mountain: "I admire you!" The voice answers: "I admire you!"

Again, the man screams: "You are a champion!" The voice answers: "You are a champion!"

The boy is surprised, but does not understand. Then, the father explains: "People call this echo, but really this is life. It gives you back everything you say or do. Our life is simply a reflection of our actions. If you want more love in the world, create more love in your heart."

He went on, "If you want more competence in your team, improve your competence. This relationship applies to everything, in all aspect of life; life will give you back everything you have given to it."

Your life is not a coincidence. It is a reflection of you and what you put into it. The same could be said about finding forgiveness.

Addiction. Alcoholism. Self-hatred. They are just a few products of not knowing how to forgive yourself for the things that people might have done, or things that you have done to other people. Yet, what about when you have done something wrong to yourself? How do you deal with it?

When we have done something wrong to other people, we may feel so overwhelmed with our guilt that we begin to punish ourselves in whatever way possible for what we did. We may even try to apologize profusely to the person that we have wronged, but never do we ever apologize to ourselves. Not even once.

I have mentioned several times that you cannot forgive other people until you have forgiven yourself. You deserve forgiveness before you forgive anyone. You always will.

Believe me; we all have played the blame game with ourselves. You might blame yourself for not doing more when a loved one was in trouble. You might blame yourself for the hurt you suffered at the hands of another.

You may find yourself saying, "How could I have been so stupid!" Instead of, "I need to apologize to myself for allowing myself to go through that or having allowed that to happen." When you apologize to yourself, you again are not letting the other person off the hook for hurting you.

It is a reminder that they are human just like you are. They made a mistake, just like you could have. You cannot always live your life begging for another person's forgiveness or wallowing in your guilt either.

Even when you make a mistake, you cannot spend the rest of your life blaming yourself all over again, for what you may have done. At that point, it's not what you did or what happened, but how you responded to it.

Here's a good example...The day my grandfather died, I saw him at the front door of the apartment that he shared with my grandmother. I was dropping off my cousin, who I had taken to the movies. He made a remark about how quickly the time had passed. I waved and that was the last time I saw him alive.

That night I got the phone call that he had had a heart attack. I kept asking myself if only I had stayed a little longer. If I could have seen something, I could have helped. I could have...done nothing more than I did.

That's the hard part. You always will ask yourself what if. What could I have done? The greatest thing that you can do for yourself in a case like that is to realize that there is nothing that you can do.

We cannot turn back the hands of time. We cannot predict the future. So what more can we do when bad things occur? It is simple; you can admit your limitations. Sometimes, that's your only response. You can't be all things to all people, all of the time. I put my trust in God to be there when I cannot be.

I have learned that guilt like that, based on your feelings of being powerless, is common.

Yet, when you realize your limitations and are honest about it, you will realize that that guilt should not exist.

As any doctor, police officer, nurse, firefighter, or even lifeguard knows, you cannot save everyone. Still other times, a person has to try to save themselves; you did just that in buying this book. When you have done something wrong, you need to admit it.

I am going to share, in a few moments, with you, how to apologize to ensure that people around you know that you are sincere and forgive in a way that will show others that you are sincere to them, and even, yourself.

However, first, I need you to remember that true healing cannot begin until you ease that sense of self-doubt, sense of failure and let go of the guilt that you feel. Your past only describes you; it does not define who you are or what you can become.

If not, you will continue to wallow in that unresolved hurt and pain. You have one of two choices when it comes to pain, either you learn to deal with it, or you find some way to ease it. When it is physical pain, you will need to see a doctor. For emotional pain, I choose forgiveness. What about you?

Right now, you are at a serious crossroads in your life. You can either choose to live your life or you can let life live you but you cannot do both. You can't.

You can allow yourself to become consumed by the problems in your life or you can deal with them head on. It's your choice. Problems will not go away on their own. Your life is what you make it.

If you put misery into your life through your words, your actions, or your association with the wrong people, what do you expect to get out of it? Water seeks its own level. If you want the best, you have to seek out the best.

That's the same thing that can be said about forgiveness. Nobody should ever have to earn it. Just like respect, it must be given to be received. If anybody has to earn it, then why would they ever need it?

Therefore, in the end, in order to get respect, you must give respect. In order to get forgiveness, you must give forgiveness. The problem is, with forgiveness, people only put in it what they think people deserve and often, it is not very much...

Forgiveness Is What You Make It...

I keep saying over and over again that forgiveness is the key. There is a good reason for that, it is good for you. Forgiveness is that moment when you stop worrying about what somebody did to you and focus on loving yourself and being there for you.

If you still feel you cannot forgive anyone, I want you to think about the one man in this world that my grandmother contends is better than all of us. They talked about him, ridiculed him, and considered him crazy, yet, she always mentions him.

My grandmother always said this when somebody mentioned that somebody was "talking" about them. When someone mentions someone doing anything that would be considered crazy, she always mentions him. Who was this man? Jesus Christ.

Even Jesus, as he hung there on the cross, knew forgiveness. In Luke 23: 34 "Then said Jesus, Father, forgive them; for they know not what they do." If Jesus could forgive those that were causing harm to him, what about you? What would you have done?

114

Even then, forgiveness is always what you put into it. If you don't give it 100%, that's usually what you will get out of it. If you only put a little bit into it, what do you expect to get out of it? Why would you allow your inability to forgive stand in your way of a better life?

Again, bad things will happen to good people but without forgiveness, we are left to pay a price for not living up to it. Any anger you might feel will be like a spark that will eventually ignite into a fire that will consume you, if you let it.

The frustration or anger that you feel at times when things are out of your control is often turned inward on yourself. You might even distance yourself from the people around you. You might end up throwing yourself into your work. What does that solve?

You might even find yourself becoming hostile towards people who have nothing to do with what is hurting you. You are having a bad day, so everyone around you has to suffer and they usually do, because of you.

How many times have you taken a bad day at work home to your family? How many times have you taken your problems with your family to work? It happens to everyone at some point.

That's why it is never good to go to bed angry. You should never let the sun set on your anger and frustration. It's what you will wake up to. You probably thought people were joking when they talk about waking up on the wrong side of the bed.

Who wants to be around a grouch? Who wants to be around someone who has built a wall around them? You think you are using that wall to protect your feelings but it is really keeping people out. It is that fear of being hurt rearing its ugly head.

That is not to be confused with the people that like to play the victim. How many times have you seen someone that you know and you asked them how they are doing? All you wanted was an "I'm fine."

They will tell you good initially, but then afterwards, they want to tell you about every bad thing that has happened since you saw them last. The car accident. The death in the family. How they lost their job.

It is easy to play the victim for some people, because they like the attention. For others, haunted by the past, they have no choice. It is all that they know. They need somebody to feel sorry for them. They want your sympathy and your empathy, not God's help.

I mentioned that misery loves company and that is what happens when you play the victim role, either by choice or by circumstance. In reality, it's not what happens to you, but how you respond to it.

People often complain about things, because there will always be somebody there to listen. Why would they listen? They are waiting their turn to tell you how bad their life is too.

If your mother passed away, so did their cousin's aunt's mother. They never mention that she passed away three years ago, but they wanted something to say.

As the victim, you will always get the attention you may, or may not, want. It is better to play the victim too. Playing the victim will always get people's sympathy. That is until people begin to avoid you.

Here comes (fill in your name.) (Fill your name) always want to tell you about how good she is even though her husband left her to raise ten kids on her own. Thank God for the kids.

They might even say (fill in your name) who had surgery six years ago but always want to tell you about her operation. She can always dance and even run a marathon any other time. People will talk, just not to you about it.

It sounds harsh, but eventually, people will get tired of you playing the victim. Everybody will, except you. Trust me; excuses only please the people that use them.

Again, misery loves company, but the only people misery attracts are people that are unhappy too. How can other people love you when you do not even love yourself?

Do not get me wrong now; you may not even know you are doing this to yourself. You may know it and want to change. Yet, there is a big difference between what you want and what you need.

What you want may not always be good for you. Playing the victim is one of them. Believe me, it never will be. I never allowed myself to learn how to play the victim. I used to ask myself why after everything in my life I did not turn to alcohol or drugs to sooth the hurt and pains that I felt in my life. What I learned was that drugs and alcohol only dull the pain. What happens when I sobered up? What happens then?

Pain is still pain. You cannot run from yourself when it comes to dealing with the problems in your life. There is nowhere to hide. Wherever you go, that is where the pain will always be. Try it. I did. You won't like it.

As a child and as an adult, I already have seen what drugs and alcohol has done to the people around me. I did not like it. Why add insult to injury by doing drugs or drinking? I find it interesting when people find out that I don't do drink, how they need to explain their drinking habits to me. You don't need to.

In life, unless asked I never explain myself. Why explain? Your true friends don't need it and if someone doesn't like you or something about you, they won't believe you any way. Some things you just don't do. Explaining unless asked is not one of them.

Nor would I apologize when other people were messing up around me. You have heard me say it several times in this book, but I think it is about time that I explain myself. I mean really explain it.

You see when I am wrong. I am wrong, even to myself, I acknowledge it. You have to. It is not a sign of weakness, but instead a sign of strength. Yet, what I won't do is to apologize for when somebody else does something wrong. That's not helping the situation.

How can anyone ever take responsibility for what they are doing wrong if you are always quick to tell them that the situation is "okay" or "alright?" How can that be?

The worst thing you can do also is to spend your life constantly worrying about what other people have done and not doing something about it. Not everything is okay. It is not.

You are strong enough to deal with your mistakes and to know when somebody has made a mistake. You always have been and always will be. It is just at times, we choose not to see things that way.

You also cannot live your life wondering if the people around you are going to hurt you. Your ex may have done this, that or the other, but you have this fear the next person is going to do the same. Not everyone does things the same way. They will not.

At this point, you need to forgive yourself for believing that all people would be like them. You need to forgive the person who hurt you for what they did and come to the conclusion that they can never hurt you again. Why? You won't allow it. Then, move on. They have, or will, when they see that you have.

Do yourself a huge favor and do not talk about them. Please stop thinking about them. Do not dwell on them and the things that they used to do. The last thing any new man in a woman's life wants to hear about, is all the things that her ex-boyfriend or husband, used to do, when the new man in her life, could become her next boyfriend or husband.

Another telltale sign that you need to apologize to yourself is that sense of sadness. It is okay to be sad sometimes, but not all the time. It's another case of playing the victim to always talk about what went wrong in your life and never finding anything good to say about anything in it.

Moping is not attractive. Angry is not a good look for anyone, except for maybe Oscar the Grouch of *Sesame Street* fame. If you tell yourself that you are unhappy, how much you want to bet you will be--unhappy.

If you tell yourself that only (the love of your life) will make you happy, you will not be happy with anyone but them. What if you cannot be with them? What if they treated you badly? What if they hurt you so?

Again, you need to remember you are not forgiving the person. You are forgiving what they did. Everyone makes mistakes even you. Everybody. The key to all of this is to forgive yourself first and do it unconditionally.

Even if you stayed with a person or in a situation you shouldn't and just now finally saw the light, do not continue to blame yourself and others for it?

Do not make excuses like you stayed because of the children. You should not kick yourself for staying; you should applaud yourself for leaving. It's a sign of strength, not weakness.

Some things you have to let go and let God handle. To all things, there is a season. There is a when, why and a how to forgiveness. I think it is about time that we talked about the "when." Trust me; it is not what you think it is…

When Is The Right Time To Forgive...

A police officer in a small town stopped a motorist who was speeding down Main Street.

"But officer," the man began, "I can explain..."

"Just be quiet," snapped the officer. "I'm going to let you cool your heels in jail until the chief gets back."

"But, officer, I just wanted to say...,"

"And I said to keep quiet! You're going to jail!"

A few hours later, the officer looked in on his prisoner and said, "Lucky for you that the chief's at his daughter's wedding. He'll be in a good mood when he gets back."

"Do not count on it," answered the fellow in the cell. "I'm the groom."

Everyone makes mistakes. We all do. In this country, we are deemed innocent until proven guilty, sometimes people are guilty. At other times, things always seem to come to the light to prove someone's innocence.

Nobody gets everything right all the time. We all fail at something and that is the moment when you have to pick yourself back up and try again. I do.

Again, your past describes you; it tells you where you have been. It doesn't define you, by telling you who you are or what you can become. You will do that.

With forgiveness though, what you cannot do means exactly what you will not do? The minute you open your mouth to tell a person that you cannot forgive them, it is the same as telling them that you will not forgive them.

We always hear what a person cannot do faster than we hear what they can do. If I were around, anyone who says this, I would have asked why not? I usually will ask.

That is what forgiveness is, something has gone wrong, and you have to find the means to move on. The million-dollar question that most people ask is when the right time to forgive anyone?

I always say when something has gone wrong. Why wait? Do you ever wait when you get a bad cut? You do not want to wait until it gets worst. That's why you should forgive early and forgive often. It's not what happens to you, but how you respond to it.

I would suggest that you do not wait for the other person to offer up an apology either. That is because no matter what happened between you two, you played your part in it.

We will talk about that as well. Yet, I'd also suggest that you give the person some time to calm down and let their emotions settle, before you go back and talk to them.

The person, or anyone else, will never expect you to come back so soon. This also is apart of the answer of how long should you wait. You are still doing it when everyone doubts it cannot be done.

How many times have you heard a person say after they saw two people fight, "You will not be seeing those two together for awhile!"

That is a true test of anyone's strengths, when the doubts still exist. When people count you out not be able to do anything is when you should. Did you know that?

Knowing what my mother told me about my education, after she passed away, many people said, he is not going to college. I even stopped going to school for a month in my senior year of high school because I was always getting in trouble.

Well, four college degrees including two Master degrees later, I am can safely say they were wrong. I am glad to say I was not the only one counted out by what I could not do. Did you know that...

Beethoven, the famous composer, was told by his music teacher that as a composer, he was hopeless. Guess that was not music to any one who has heard his music's ears?

Walt Disney, the famous cartoonist, was fired by a newspaper because he had "no good ideas." Guess he "showed" them not if he was a man or a mouse, but that he was the better man with a mouse.

Thomas Edison, the famous inventor, was told by his teacher that he was too stupid to learn anything. Is that when the light bulb went off in his head?

Albert Einstein, the brilliant scientist, was four years old before he spoke. He stuttered until he was nine. He was considered mentally retarded. He was advised to drop out of high school and was told by his teachers that he would never amount to much. Guess who got the last laugh.

Henry Ford's first two automobile businesses failed. Yes, that Henry Ford. Have you driven a Ford lately?

Michael Jordan, considered by some to be the greatest basketball player of all time, was actually cut from his high school basketball team. How many NBA championship rings does Jordan have?

William H. Macy's store failed seven times before it caught on. The whole block of 34th Street in New York is proof of what his dreams are really made of.

Babe Ruth, the legendary baseball player, struck out 1,330 times, but he also hit 714 home runs. You cannot win them all. We all make mistakes.

Stephen Spielberg, who hasn't seen one of his movies from "Jaws" to "E.T.", dropped out of high school as a sophomore. Spielberg was persuaded to come back and was placed in a learning-disabled class. He lasted a month and here you thought Indian Jones, one of his characters, had an adventure.

Ray Kroc, the force behind McDonald's restaurants, failed as a real estate salesperson before discovering the idea for McDonald's. Maybe his detractors can have some fries to go along with eating crow.

Then, there is the person who is holding this book right now, who people thought could never find forgiveness. You might have even doubted it yourself. Again, maybe you were not ready to begin the process until now.

With forgiveness, what you cannot do means what you will not do? There is no exact time to apologize or offer forgiveness to anyone. The moment that you make up your mind to forgive someone, also make the effort to see it through to the end, no matter what.

You may not always get the same results with forgiveness. It is not always about the journey with forgiveness, it is about the destination. You have to try to try again until you get it right.

With the Amish, forgiveness may have come before the slight ever occurred. I know when you read it; you were probably surprised by that. How can a person be forgiven before a person does something?

The Amish truly believe that God's forgiveness of them is dependent on their extending forgiveness to other people. They do not seek revenge but ask for forgiveness for the wrongdoer. Keep in mind that we all do something wrong in our lives.

The question is when we do something wrong, do we want people to forgive us? That is why we should always forgive others. Again, how can we begin to heal that which we don't want to acknowledge?

With the Amish understanding of forgiveness, you should know that it is a long process. It is difficult. It is a painful experience replacing bitter feelings towards someone.

It is something that takes time. Even the Amish would say that, even that happens only through God's grace, with the faith that the emotional forgiveness will follow over months and years. It should be done though.

They do not begin with trying to blame someone, or something. It is like not questioning how some milk was spilled but seeing the problem and working to clean it up. Everyone involved must do this.

No fingers are pointed. No blame is laid on anyone. No one is angry or upset. No one walks away feeling at ill ease.

It goes back to that idea that you cannot love anybody until you have loved yourself. You cannot truly expect to be forgiven, unless you truly know how to forgive others.

As with anything in life, we do not always need a reason to take that faithful first step. Some things should be done as easy as breathing. One of those things should be forgiveness.

Often, when we reach the moment of forgiveness, needing to forgive. It is usually because the outwards signs of our inner pain begin to show. We are depressed, we are overly anxious. We are feeling hate or anger. We might be consumed with regret.

There are those that begin to withdraw into themselves. They cut off friends and family. If people would take a moment and be honest with themselves,

I mean start to tell the truth about everything, it could change everything. When the time comes, here's what you should do...

When The Time Comes...

The first thing you need to know when it comes to truly dealing with your pain is honesty. When you are so consumed with anger and rage, you should know its time to seek forgiveness and if need be, someone to talk to, like a counselor or a spiritual advisor, who can help channel your emotions.

When that time comes, you have to be honest about what happened and what needs to be done. Do you want to remain bitter and angry or do you really want to learn how to get past it? It is time to move on.

It is not the time to deny guilt. There is no time to pretend that it did not happen or plan to deal with it another time. That despair you feel is a result of your unconscious need to deal with your pain. Only your honesty will heal your pain. You need closure.

The same way when you read a book and you come to the end, you close it. You will always remember what happened in the story, but you will not be as emotionally invested as when you first read it.

To do this, you need to learn to air out your feelings when they occur. Depression is often anger turned inward. If someone has hurt you, it is okay to let them know. You are not a child anymore, who is supposed to speak when spoken to and only with permission.

Some people value your silence. Silence is often looked upon as consent. If you do not speak up and out, they will assume that that is what you wanted for them to do. Again, you did not say anything.

It does not help you to have something on your mind and not speak on it. The other side of this is when somebody asks you directly if there is something on your mind. You may say you do not want to talk about it.

It is okay to think things over, or find the right way to say something. Take your time. If you do not speak up, your silence hurts you and everyone else involved. When things go wrong and you do not want to talk about it, you are actually hurting whatever relationship the problem is in.

How? Let us say you are a wife and you find out that your husband is cheating. If you do not confront it head on, you are hurting that relationship. You can deny it is happening right up to the divorce. You will, in deed.

If you find out that your son, or daughter, is doing drugs and you do not say anything about it, you are hurting that relationship. The problem will not clear up on its own. Are you waiting for the funeral to speak on it?

I know that it sounds very harsh, but we are being honest. That's the first step in dealing with a problem. Be honest, very honest.

The problem is that whenever an issue such as infidelity, or even some thing like drug or alcohol abuse, rears its head in a family, we tend to accept responsibility for it as if we put the problem in the person's hands. If we ignore it, we may be just as guilty.

In a situation like that, you tend to feel like you drove them to drink. You drove them to cheat. They may have told you that you did. You may have come up with that on your own. Why? How? When?

If you accept that kind of blame, what part did they play in all of that? What did they do? There may be a deeper issue there that an intervention may help supersede. Otherwise, the person will always blame other people for their problems and their pain.

It is easier to lay blame than accept responsibility for the things that they do. They have to find some excuse for why they did what they did, or why they do what they do. You are often an easy target.

When they do accept responsibility for what they did, they have to be willing to do what they need to do to make things right. They need to accept the fact that they can't change what has already happened, but they can decide what will happen in the future.

Listen, we all have problems. Who does not have problems in their lives? Who has not had some issue that they have had to face down? Everybody has problems, issues, or concerns. Everyone.

The difference is in how we deal with it. That is the moment when you need to remind yourself you cannot accept responsibility every time someone you love messes up.

If you always take it on the chin when somebody blames you for their issues, it could be your parents, friends, or even your boss, you become an enabler.

It is because you care so much about them that you allow them to add to your baggage and all they have is a knapsack. Where is the responsibility for that?

When a person usually hears about an enabler, it is usually a wife, who knows that her husband is an alcoholic, but she still buys him alcohol for fear that he will be angry with her. He may even become angry or violent.

To me, an enabler is anyone who supports a person's bad habit no matter how bad the situation gets. You are not helping the person. You are actually robbing the person of their ability to tell right from wrong, in what they are actually doing. Never do that!

Yes, I know some issues are medical. Some people have mental or emotional issues that bring about how they resolve their problems, I know. Yet, help is available, if people choose to accept it, for whatever ails you or them. Be it emotionally, spiritually, or physically, but you have to ask for it.

The truth is we can't handle everything on our own. It doesn't matter if the issue is affecting you or someone that you love. If you had a medical issue, you wouldn't try to handle it on your own.

Why not treat the anger, guilt, hurt or emotional pain that you sometimes feel with the same kind of consideration? There is no shame in seeking help for any problem, big or small.

With any kind of help though, as the person involved, for whatever reason, you have to first know that you need help. Then, when you seek it out, you also have also to adhere to the help that you are given.

That simply means listening to the advice reputable people, such as therapists, are offering you and you have to use it. The problem is though that not everybody is ready to seek help, though. The best way to be able to tell a person needs help, is when confronted with a problem, they tend to rationalize it.

They have an excuse for everything that they do. They claim that they can always stop when they want to. They don't have a problem. Denial isn't just a river in Egypt.

That son, that is doing drugs, is not experimenting because he is young. The cheating spouse is not just having a fling. Their problems are very real and ignoring it, justifying it, or rationalizing it, do not help the situation, or them, at all.

The only way that a problem can get better is when you deal with it. Think about a cut, before you put that band-aid on it and you have cleaned things up, it is going to hurt some more before it gets better. You have to deal with it.

Maybe, you are so gripped by fear that you do not want to deal with it. As if you will only make matters worst. What happens if you don't deal with it? You will only end up with a case of what if. That's the point where things have gone from bad to worst.

Nevertheless, you need to do it right away. If there ever was a time to deal with any problem in your life, the time is now. The number one question for you, now, is how?

As with any thing, there is a right and wrong way to do anything. There is a secret to forgiveness and apologies, beyond even saying sorry. You will have to make sure that you have done it the right way, for it to count.

So far, we have talked about the who, what and when with forgiveness, let me introduce you to the how...

True Apologies and "A Pile Of Lies"...

They say it is easier to ask for forgiveness than to ask for permission. Most people never will think to apologize until after they are caught and face punishment, or it is too late to change something that happened. If they did, they would not do it.

Even then, they believe that a little lie will not hurt anyone. I personally hate lying. Why lie when the truth will do? It is so easy to tell a lie for some people.

Regardless of the effect it will have on another person, it is easier to lie than to tell the truth for some people.

If a person is willing to lie to himself, or herself, and God what makes you think they will not lie to you? At some point, we all have told a lie in our lives.

We could have said that it was 12 o'clock when it was only 11:58. You might not think it is a lie, but for some people, it is not the truth. Did you ever think about that.

Again, if a person will lie to God and themselves, what makes you think they will not lie to you? If they will lie to you about something small, how can you be sure that when they have apologized that they really mean it? How do you know?

Next to love, sorry is one of the most overused words in the world. They say it and then, nothing happens. Maybe that is why it is so easy for them to hurt you again.

When a person apologizes, it should never be used as a way to avoid guilt. If anything, a true apology will free you from that guilt. To some people, sorry is just what needs to be said before they do something wrong.

Sorry, I am going to have to break up with you. Sorry, I cannot make the party. Sorry, but I am going to have to call you back. It may not seem like something serious, but just you wait. You will see.

A sincere apology is not only key to repairing damaged relationships but is the means that we have to maintain strong ones.

What then is a sincere apology? A sincere apology always shows that you, in some way, shape and form, actually regret what you did and are trying to make an effort to make things right, if that is possible, for what was done. It is almost biblical; it should come without conditions or repercussions.

A sincere apology is not just a way to end an argument. An apology should never be your way of introducing a negative action. Sorry, but I am going to have to let you go from your job. They think that a sorry will just ease their guilt, when it only adds to yours.

Accepting responsibility is a huge step in securing and repairing any relationship. Often as parents, many of the conversations that we have with our children are based on because you said so. If you said it, it has to be. That's what our parents told us.

Why do we do some things? Nine times out of ten, we got it from our family. Remember sins of the father, and mother, for that matter, does not rest on the heads of their children, they are taught. What will your children learn from you? You'd be surprise what they already have learned from you.

Here's a clear example of that...I once heard the story of a woman who cut the ends off her ham when she cooked it. She did this every time. One day her daughter asked her why she did it. She said her mother always did it. Even then, she didn't know why.

The woman immediately called her mother and asked her mother why she always cut the ends off her ham. The mother did not hesitate to say her own mother always did it.

Puzzled by the mystery, she decided to call her mother. On a three-way call, the women asked the older woman why she always cut the ends off her ham when she cooked it.

The other women explained that the granddaughter now did it because her mother did it. Now all of the women cut the ends off her ham, because they had seen her mother do it. All except the original woman.

Now after years and years, they were going to get to the bottom of all of this so they called her. The oldest woman laughed at the question that they had asked her.

Her response. She simply said that there was only one reason why she cut the ends off her ham, the pan was too small for her to fit the ham in without cutting it.

Think about it this way, we tend to say sorry when something happens because it's what we have been taught just like cutting the ends of the hams. It is what we know to do.

What happens when you have never been taught the true reason why?

Ezekiel 18:14 tells us "Now if he has a son who see all of his father's sins, which he has done and considers and does not such like."

Again, in order for you to understand what ails you, you must find out the moment in life, when someone, or something, has failed you. It is only then that you can begin to heal.

That's because, in finding forgiveness, when you apologize, you put yourself one-step closer to being forgiven for what you did.

In turn, remembering that you played a part in what happened, you will find the opportunity find forgiveness for other people.

Apologizing and meaning may take some time. That is why I always suggest that people start with themselves. It could mean the difference between a person who apologizes and one who offers "a pile of lies."

You know the lies, the person says they are sorry but they do something wrong all over again. There is a reason the person can't apologize and mean it; their ego is standing in their way and it is hurting them...

Pride Comes Before A Fall...

"Well, you shouldn't have said what you said..." Have you ever heard this from someone? You know this type of person; it might be you, when confronted with the truth.

This kind of person is quick to say "well, you should not have done what you did." That's why they did what they did. Stop thinking like that right now. You are not helping anyone.

For others, some people just cannot handle the truth. Therefore, they cannot find forgiveness. They think that if they apologize then whatever that they say that they did wrong will be held against them.

Think about what happens when you do not apologize. What will people think of you then? They will think you cannot accept responsibility. You are going to have to let your ego go and put your pride aside and apologize. Forgive and then, you too can be forgiven.

You cannot be afraid of what people think of you after you apologize. You have to trust in yourself that you are doing the right thing. You are planting the seeds of your future with each apology. Take the story of Honi and the carob tree…

One day when Honi, the righteous man, was out walking, he came upon a man planting a carob tree. Honi watched as he carried out his work. The man dug a hole for the roots of the small tree and then carefully put the tree in the hole and patted soil all around it.

Afterwards, he gave it some water from a nearby stream. "How long will it be before this tree bears fruit?" Honi asked.

"Seventy years," the man replied. "How do you know you'll be alive in seventy years?"

"Just as I found carob trees when I came into the world," answered the man, "so I am now planting carob trees for my grandchildren to enjoy."

Honi pondered this important idea. He understood that not everything we do in our lifetime has immediate results. Sometimes the fruit of our actions don't become obvious for many years afterwards. The same thing might be said about forgiveness.

Yet, even if forgiveness will not bring immediate results, but it will bring results, that you will be able to see and feel eventually. So with that said, how do you apologize and make it count? There are five parts to a sincere apology. Five.

There should first be the actual words that "I apologize." Not sorry, once you are sorry, you are always sorry. Sorry implies misery and you are trying to make things better.

The second part, you should state what you are apologizing for. Be honest. Be open. Do not explain why you did what you did. Remember that your friends do not need it and your enemies will not believe you any way. Why should they?

Most people, who try to explain what happened, they will only turn that apology into another argument. That is because the feelings that brought on the problem will resurface.

In the heat of the moment, the temptation is there to point a finger and for you to start on what the other person did.

When a person is hurt, they do not care why you did it. In the forgiveness process, they may ask why. Just not now. Do not explain why when you are apologizing. Just state what went wrong. That is it.

Third, you should accept responsibility for what you did. There should be an offer of resolution, how you can make the situation better. What can you do?

Fourth, there should be a promise that what ever happened should not happen again. This is very important. You must follow through on this commitment to change. If you are not committed to change, then you are not really apologizing. You are offering up "a pile of lies."

Lastly, never ask for a person's forgiveness at the end. You will not get it. Do you forgive me? That is not a sign of sincerity you just want to end the situation the best way you know how. That's not the best way to do it.

Why not just tell the person to stop acting like that and make them mad from the start? You know that is an easy way to start a fight. Your apology wasn't sincere; it was to get a result.

When you apologize, you should know that the person might get up and walk away when talking face to face. They have every right to. On a call, they may just hang up the phone.

They may not say anything at all. That is the worst that can happen.

One of the good things that might happen is that they will apologize to you as well. They may just give you a hug and say nothing else. Everyone behaves differently. It's never easy and it's never cut and dry.

The minute that you begin to apologize it should be sincere. Take your time. Remember you are righting a wrong and not trying to hurt anyone any further, especially not yourself. People can spot a fake apology. That is like adding insult to injury.

Again, you are trying to right a wrong and not add salt to the wound. It should not come with any stipulations. Let's try it out. Here's a simple situation where an apology will take you a long way.

Let's say you stayed out late and forgot to tell someone like your spouse, or significant other, that you would be late. Do not tell them that you are sorry that they are upset. Try something like:

"I apologize for being late. I know I should have called if I was going to be late. I know I forgot to call in the past. I will try to remember to call in the future. Is there anything you need me to do now that I am here?" Please mean everything that you say.

Forgiveness works the same way. Okay, not exactly. With that said, I know you are wondering so how do you forgive someone and make it count? There are five steps.

However, first I need you to do something for me. I need you to stop and think about a time when you have ever said "I forgive you" to somebody aloud or in a letter. Chances are you cannot. It does not mean that you cannot or you haven't forgiven anyone.

With forgiveness, you usually will not even say it aloud unless somebody asks for it. You do have to acknowledge it. Imagine how you would feel, wrecked with guilt if someone does not know you genuinely did not mean to do something.

As I said before, some people may never forgive a person for what they did. I cannot say that that is a good thing, but it happens.

Remember forgiveness is about you and for you. It may help the other person but until you can forgive yourself and others for what occurred, you will not be able to move on.

If you want to truly forgive someone, treat it just like you would treat an apology again. Okay, so where were we? There are five parts to a sincere apology. Five.

There should first be the actual words that "I forgive you." The second part, you should state what you are forgiving the person for. This is a key step that ensures that you are acknowledging that you were wronged.

The third is to remind the person that they will not be allowed to hurt you again in any way. Some people will try again, trust me. Let them know that they can't. Fourth, you have a right to tell them how you felt when you have been wronged.

Lastly, you also have a right to tell them what you need to do next. Maybe you need time; maybe you need them to do something like leave you alone for a while.

Here is the same situation about being late, but instead you are on the forgiving end of things: "I forgive you for being late in coming home. I am not going to allow you to keep upsetting me by not calling, or keeping me up waiting for you. You had me worried that something might have happened. Right now,

I need you to call me the next time you know you are going to be late."

Admitting how you felt is a big step. Many of us do not want to admit when we have been hurt. They treat being hurt with being a victim. Who wants to be a victim?

Nevertheless, you have to remember that bad things happen to good people. Remember what I said, you have to be completely honest. For some people they will never admit that they are guilty.

When some people forgive, they may never even let the person know. Then, they wonder why the continued relationship continues to remain strained. The forgiveness remains between them and God. It's enough for them to let God know and not the person being forgiven. That isn't fair to you. Here's why…

If somebody forgave you, would you want to know? Yet, for others, a part of their ability to forgive and end the hurting process and begin to heal, they have to let a person know just how they feel.

I did just that when I put pen to page and wrote my father that letter when I was just nineteen, after his arrest during his drug addiction. For some people, you may write a similar letter. You need let it out in some way.

Even then, it's not the actual response of the person that even matters; it is the not having to hold it inside that counts more. You have lightened your burden and you unpacked some of your excessive baggage.

Remember what I said, not everybody will come to you to apologize for what a person did. That may make forgiveness harder than it already is. Is it impossible? The answer is no. The hardest part of forgiveness is trying to understand why people did what they did. In the end, we may never know.

I have learned that you should never ask a question that you are not spiritually, or emotionally, prepared for the answer. I never go where I am not invited. Sometimes, that place, which you should not get into, is questioning why someone did anything.

You may actually be doing more harm than good by seeking answers when in reality, it might be better to focus on the act of forgiveness and not what was actually done. It's time that we talk about why that is...

The Second Most Powerful
Lesson That I Have Ever Learned...

Before I go on, I need to share something else with you. As I said before, bad things will happen to everyone, including me. You might still feel violated or angry. I sometimes do.

For me, it happened on November 17th, 2007, when an excessive knocking came at my front door and it awakened me from my sleep. It was the first time that I wish I did not even open my door. It was about my brother.

On his way to see the girlfriend that he had just started dating, my brother was murdered. He was shot and killed. To this day, we do not know why. All I still think about was my brother laying there on the concrete of someone's sidewalk alone.

My brother was dead because someone did not love my brother enough, or stopped to think that others did, truly love him and they killed him. They shot him and left him to die alone in the streets. That day my entire family became the victim of his murder.

Try having to explain to a sister that had already lost her mother, an uncle, and a grandfather suddenly, that now her brother was dead. It was the worst day of my life.

Try explaining to a grandmother that her oldest grandson was murdered. What about his daughters? How do you explain to a little girl, my youngest niece was not even five years old, that her father was gone? How?

At the funeral, my grandmother then stood before the church, filled with people from wall to wall. She said something that shocked everyone in the room. It shocked me.

My grandmother said that if the person that killed her grandson, my brother, was in the room that she forgave them. All she asked was that they turn themselves in.

At the time, I was too numb with grief to understand it. I was hurt. I was too focused on my loss that forgot about everybody else around me at times. In that moment, all I could think about was that I lost my brother.

When people die, we only think of our pain. We never consider that other people may be hurting too. We never think of the person and truly celebrate their lives. We are so focused on our loss of them. Not that they passed on.

For my brother, the murderer, to date, has never been caught. He, or she, never turned himself, or herself, in. My faith in God remains firm that he will bring my brother's killer to justice. That is the second most powerful lesson that I have ever learned.

It is when you let go of that need to get even; it allows God the opportunity to have the "last laugh." Vengeance is mine, I will recompense sayeth the Lord. Let God have his say!

If you are so fixated on doing your job of getting even, then what is there left for God to do? You may challenge this and say well, God has not done anything to the person, but the question is how do you know?

Trust me, as someone who has loved and lost in life, the pain is there. Nevertheless, what are you going to do about it? I understand that kind of pain. I understand the who, the what, the when, the where and the why of the pain of not knowing.

When somebody has harmed your family, you often want to make the person and their family suffer the same way. In the case of Charles Roberts, there was no way to make him suffer more than he already did. What about his family? They did not deserve that.

Surely, his wife should have seen the signs of something being wrong. They had breakfast and then walked their children to the school bus stop before she left for bible study that morning.

All of the warning signs were there. Their daughter had died after all nine years before. Somebody had to see it! Let us be honest, unless we learn to read minds, how was anyone to know what Roberts would do?

When tragedies, such as what happened to the Amish, occur, the news media often interviews those closest to them. It is a very rare occasion if somebody ever comes forth and tells you that they always knew there was something wrong. If they did, why didn't they do something to stop it?

Sure, some people will ignore the signs of a problem, but not everybody. What if it was the reverse and your family member did something to someone else? You would probably be too embarrassed to say anything to the other family.

Often, the only time that you would ever hear a person ever apologize for what they did to a family is at that person's sentencing. Yes, I said family because when you harm a person you are harming the whole family.

When does a family ever step forward and apologize for the actions of their family member? As I said, you will not hear anything from the family of the man or woman that has harmed your family. Often, they are too busy justifying what happened or making excuses for what occurred or will claim the person did not do it. The truth hurts.

With Charles Roberts, did you really think that Charles Roberts' wife had the strength to reach out to the Amish families? She was dealing with her own grief. She had to explain to her own children what happened. She had to pick up the pieces of her own life.

That is why the Amish proved to be people far greater than anyone can imagine. They went to her instead and offered their support. They did not point fingers, and they did not play the blame game. That would have been too easy. That would have done more harm than good. They offered her forgiveness.

When a person is hurt, again, they do not care why a person did it. They do not. The one thing I learned is that pain does not stem from another person's love. It is pain.

How else could you explain all of the bad in the world? It has to come from somewhere. Even then, sometimes, we have to endure that pain to know what is not right.

The worst lesson that somebody can ever teach is to teach pain through neglect and abuse. It becomes a vicious cycle. For millions of people, not every prison comes with a set of bars. We create our own.

When someone hurts you, you turn around and hurt somebody else. What do you get from that? It could be your spouse, friend, a relative, or your children. In some cases, you will even hurt a stranger.

Remember that the sins of the father do not rest on the heads of his children; it has been taught to them. How else can you explain why a boy who saw his father abuse his mother is more likely to abuse the women in his life?

I know that we cannot change what happens; we can choose how we respond to it. All the while, we give God room to exact the true form of justice. In the forgiveness process, you may ask why a person did what they did. However, in forgiveness, you are letting go of the pain of what they did.

Nevertheless, you have to acknowledge that the pain does exist. Every detail and every part, acknowledge it, especially when you know who has hurt you. Sometimes, it helps even when you do not.

If they took something from you, you should let them know that they hurt you. It could be a crucial step in your own healing process. This is the time when writing a letter becomes key because it gives you time to reflect on what they did.

Even if they do not read it, at least you got it off your chest. Nine times out of ten, they will read it, because they are curious as to what you have to say. They want to know. Face to face, they may get angry and upset but in a letter, it often gives them time to reflect.

Just saying that you forgive someone, the words will not ease your pain. It will still hurt. You have to know what you are forgiving them for in the first place. Writing the letter will definitely bring emotions to the surface.

Remember you may need to seek out the support of someone you can trust to talk about it. Do so. Do not be afraid to take that step. Above all, be honest with yourself about what is happening.

When a person lied to you, maybe it was time for you to see the person for who they really are. You are not seeing them as who you wanted them to be. You are seeing them for who they really are.

If that were not the case, then you would have gone on letting them lie to you. Never allow yourself to play the victim, because as a victim you are powerless to change your circumstances when in reality, through forgiveness, you are.

In any situation, remember that you always played a part. Know the role that you played so that you know what you may have to own up to, take responsibility for and/or what you might need to do to make things right.

Remember; do not justify your behavior either. You should not let any one to do it either until the lines of communication have been reopened. It is only then that the both of you can discuss what either of you did without hurt or anger.

When they do open up, you need to do so as well. Be completely honest. You need to allow them to express why they did what they did. You need to listen without interrupting them, even if and when they are talking about the role that they think that you played. You will have your turn.

Even then, do not point fingers. Speak your mind respectfully when the time comes. You both should accept responsibility for what happened. There should be an offer of resolution. How both of you can make the situation better?

If they do not know about this, teach them. Give them a copy of this book. Forgiveness should be on both of your parts. Just saying that you are sorry is not enough. What will both of you do to make it better?

Again, there should be a promise that what occurred should not be repeated. This is a commitment to change. Remember that change comes with forgiveness and will happen with you, or without you.

If you are not committed to change, you are not really apologizing, you are offering up, again, "a pile of lies." That is not the hard part though. It is at that moment that you have big decision to make.

At that moment, you must decide if the person is worth having in your life or has the time come to move on without them....

Letting In...

Not everyone from your past should remain there. Here is an example...The brand new pastor and his wife, newly assigned to their first ministry, to reopen a church in urban Brooklyn, arrived in early October excited about their opportunities.

When they saw their church, it was very run down and needed much work. They set a goal to have everything done in time to have their first service on Christmas Eve.

They worked hard, repairing pews, plastering walls, painting, and etc. By December 18th, they were ahead of schedule and just about finished. On December 19th, a terrible tempest, a driving rainstorm, hit the area, and lasted for two days. On the 21st, the pastor went over to the church.

His heart sunk when he saw that the roof had leaked, causing a large area of plaster about 6 feet by 8 feet to fall off the front wall of the sanctuary just behind the pulpit, beginning about head high.

The pastor cleaned up the mess on the floor, and not knowing what else to do but postpone the Christmas Eve service, headed home. On the way, he noticed that a local business was having a flea market type sale for charity so he stopped in. One of the items was a beautiful, hand-made, ivory colored, crocheted tablecloth with exquisite work, fine colors, and a cross-embroidered right in the center. It was truly Heaven sent!

It was just the right size to cover up the hole in the front wall. He bought it and headed back to the church. By this time, it had started to snow. An older woman running from the opposite direction was trying to catch the bus. She missed it.

The pastor invited her to wait in the warm church for the next bus 45 minutes later. She sat in a pew and paid no attention to the pastor while he got a ladder, hangers, etc. to put up the tablecloth as a wall tapestry.

The pastor could hardly believe how beautiful it looked and it covered up the entire problem area. Then, he noticed the woman walking down the center aisle towards him.

"Pastor," she asked, "Where did you get that tablecloth?" The pastor explained. The woman asked him to check the lower right corner to see if the initials, EBG had been crocheted into the right corner. They were.

These were the initials of the woman, and she had made this tablecloth 35 years before, in Austria.

The woman could hardly believe it as the pastor told how he had just bought the tablecloth. The woman explained that before the war, she and her husband were well-to-do people in Austria.

When the Nazis came, she was forced to leave. Her husband was going to follow her the next week. She had been captured. She was then sent to prison. She never saw her husband or her home again.

The pastor wanted to give her the tablecloth; but, she made the pastor keep it for the church. The pastor insisted on driving her home, which was the least he could do. She lived on the other side of Staten Island and was only in Brooklyn for the day for a house-cleaning job. She agreed.

On Christmas Eve, what a wonderful service they had. The church was almost full. The music and the spirit were great. At the end of the service, the pastor and his wife greeted everyone at the door and many said that they would return.

One older man, whom the pastor recognized from the neighborhood, continued to sit in one of the pews and stare, and the pastor wondered why he was not leaving.

The man asked him where he got the tablecloth on the front wall because it was identical to one that his wife had made years ago when they lived in Austria before the war. How could there be two tablecloths so much alike?

He told the pastor how the Nazis came, how he forced his wife to flee for her safety, and he was supposed to follow her, but he was arrested and put in a concentration camp.

He never saw his wife or his home again for all of the 35 years in between. He thought that she had given up on him. Maybe, she had died. He never knew what happened to her. In the end, he gave up looking for her.

The pastor asked him to allow him to take the man for a little ride. They drove to Staten Island and to the same house where the pastor had taken the woman three days earlier. He helped the man climb the three flights of stairs to the woman's apartment, knocked on the door and he saw the greatest Christmas reunion he could ever imagine.

Everyone loves to see someone that they deeply cared about; especially when the person is someone, they have not seen for some time. Yet, even when things did not go very well the last time you saw them, there is also a longing to see them.

What if things did not end on a good note? You might feel that feeling of fight or flight upon seeing them. It could be anyone from a parent, to an ex, or even an old friend.

Many times when we see these people, we find ourselves mentally and emotionally in the same moment that they left us last.

If you were a child and you "ran away" from or just left home the first chance you could, going home can be hard. Very hard. The difference is you cannot deal with your family the way that you did before. You just cannot.

You may have been a child when something bad happened. On the other hand, you could have just been younger and more naïve than you are now.

Nevertheless, either way, you should know and trust that you are older now and wiser than you were before. Show them.

Just like the old saying goes, you can never step into the same river twice. The water that you stepped in a moment ago, a year ago or even twenty years ago has already moved down stream. This should be a metaphor for your life; you are not the same person. So now what? What do you do about it?

Not everybody in your past should always remain there. They should not. You have changed, then, you should give some people a chance to change.

Give yourself a chance to see and to show them just how much that is. You both will probably be surprised.

Remember, we all inflict pain at one point or another. Remember what I said about not being entirely innocent in some situations. It is time that we talk about just why that is.

If you truly want to allow somebody back into your heart, there is something that you should also know. This forgiveness is not free. There is a price tag even for you for your forgiveness...

The Price Tag Of Forgiveness...

Someone once said that if you are not a part of the solution, then you must be apart of the problem. What happens if the problem continues to be you? I think I should have told you something before that forgiveness comes with a price tag. It is called honesty. Wait a minute, I think I already did.

Yet, whenever two people look at any situation there will always be something that the other misses. It is not that either of them is lying, it is just that we all see things differently from time to time.

In reality, the other person seeing what we missed might help us see the situation more clearly. There is never a better chance to understand this than when somebody has hurt us, or when, they think that they have.

It's very easily for other people see us as a victim, we give them the ammunition. When something bad happens to us, we tell the story from the point of view of being the victim. That is why I strongly suggest that you never try to justify any wrongdoing that you may have done. You did not do what you did because of what somebody did to you. You will choose what you will do.

Excuses only please the people that use them. Excuses are ranked second only to lies as the worst things that you can do. "I did this because..." "I didn't know because..." "What had happened was..." Stop right there!

Imagine hearing that from your spouse. They cheated because they felt that you neglected them. How does that sound? No, they cheated because they could. They wanted to. They had space and opportunity.

That is the problem with many people; they do what they want and then lay blame or justify it later. They are already caught. Why not just be honest about the situation? Yet, would we even want to listen? We are too busy keeping score, or at least, we used to.

I say never explain, your friends don't need it and your enemies won't believe you any way. With a friend, if you are late, they are just so glad, that you made it, to need an excuse.

If it is an enemy, even when you start to explain, they are already waiting for the lie to even suspect that what you are saying is the truth. They have already passed judgment.

With everything, there should never be a need to make somebody pay. It is this need to make somebody pay for what the person did that makes you unable to reconcile with him or her. You just want revenge.

Nine times out of ten, you are not just trying to hurt them; you have unpacked a bag and are really trying to right a past wrong. How do you know they are not suffering despite anything you can do?

If you need an explanation as to why they did what they did, wait until after the lines of communications has been opened with people that have wronged you or that you have wronged. That is time to talk about what went wrong, only then.

Yet, again, brace yourself for what you might hear. Never ask a question that you are not ready for the answer about. Maybe you did contribute to the situation. Maybe you did not. You will soon find out.

Maybe they just believed you were responsible for the situation and they blamed you and that is why they did what they did. For some of us, it will be hard to talk to the other person like this or about anything.

Think about that parent that, every holiday, uses that as an opportunity to criticize you.

Talking to them will only make you angrier than you need to be. Just as pain is pain, abuse is abuse. For you, that is what they call verbal and emotional abuse, some people just don't know what to say at times.

That is not to say that some parents will not offer constructive advice. You might have taken it the wrong way. I say constructive advice, not constructive criticism.

That is the biggest oxymoron ever, how can you build somebody up by tearing him or her down? That is something that you can't do.

A good parent offers constructive advice, like "I always loved you when you wore your hair up." Not, "If you got your hair out of your face, maybe you'd look nicer." The easiest way to stop this kind of abuse is to no longer accept, or allow it, no matter what.

If someone was to come to you and say something like, "If you got your hair out of your face, maybe you'd look nicer." You should kindly say, "Thank you, but, I prefer it this way." That is it.

Oh, that kind of remark will sting them at first. It is going to hurt them. However, it would also help them to think first before they say something to you like that.

When they counter that they were just offering advice, thank them, and repeat what you said initially. Most people do not realize that the reason why advice is often not eagerly accepted is that nobody asks for it. However, everybody wants to give it.

So now what? Here you and the person are and you are trying to rebuild the lines of communications. They are explaining what they did. Keep in mind that what they did was not entirely your fault. They did it.

If it was not even part of your fault, as in abuse, then remind them of that when it becomes your turn to talk. I know it is hard to forgive somebody if you feel what they did to you is not your fault at all, like the things that were done to you as children. Nevertheless, remember whatever was done was done by somebody that was human.

As children, we tend to look at our parents as our saviors. Mom's meals taste the best and dad is so strong. We never see our parents as being human. As human beings, we all make mistakes. That is another issue, if we keep making them and we do not see the error of our ways.

Yet, when we begin to see our parents and others as human beings that make mistakes, it becomes easier for you to see why and how that they can make mistakes just like you. They made mistakes. They will continue to make mistakes. To err is to be human, right, just as you are. I am human.

Even when the lines of communications have reopened, resist the temptation to take the bold step of asking them why they did what they did. If anything, ask them why do they "think" they did what they did.

Brace yourself for the answer. They could have been abused as well. They could have had a problematic childhood.

Whatever the case, they too may need help and you might be the first step in them getting it. When they are talking, you might find yourself revisiting the very pain that hurt you in the beginning. Take a deep breath and listen; you might learn something that you never knew before.

You do not want to wait until something bad happens, like their illness or death, before you find out these things as the son did with the son, the father, and the bible in a previous story I shared.

Do not ever forget the good times with the people that hurt you. They say a few harsh words, and suddenly, you want to kick them out of your life. Just like that, it is over.

Did you stop and think about the good times that you had? You might need to, when times get rough. It may help you and them.

No matter how bad that you think someone is, stop and think about the good things about this person. What were the good things that they did for you and to you?

It is only when the good outweighs the bad that you should consider walking away. If you cannot think of anything good about somebody you do not like now, you are lying to yourself and God.

In a relationship, if there weren't anything good about them, what attracted you to them in the first place? It will help how you see them now. If it is a family member, or someone you love, it is okay to tell them that you still love them. You just do not like the things that that person did to you.

Let them know that you will not tolerate it and if they need help, you will help them, but you will not be their victim. You are not afraid of them and will no longer allow yourself to pretend to be. I know that is a lot to think about, but, forgiveness of them is for you. They may still feel the guilt for what they did. Nevertheless, you need your peace of mind.

After you have reopened the lines of communications, it is still also okay to talk to a counselor or someone who will not be judgmental of your decision. They will give you an unbiased opinion and sounding board as you move forward in your renewed relationship.

Again, not everybody in your past should remain there, especially if it is a parent. By forgiving a parent, you are breaking a cycle of abuse that could also be affecting your children. It can lead to a better relationship for your entire family.

With others though, I have learned that there is a time to let go of the pain and the people involved. There will come a time when you will have to learn to let go and let God handle them. Just let go and let God…

Letting Go...

Before I go on, you should know that I have something that you can call a God bag. Whenever I have a problem, I write it down and I turn it over to God. I let him handle it.

No matter how big or how small. God always manages to see me through. It based on true faith. Faith is the key in handling anything. Faith tells you what you can do.

No other story that I have ever heard that underlines this message than the story of Donna. The author is unknown. It should give you some food for thought, though.

The next time you think about what you can't do, remember this story. Especially when you say, you can't forgive anyone or even yourself.

Donna's fourth grade classroom looked like many others I had seen in the past. The teacher's desk was in front and faced the students. The bulletin board featured student work.

In most respects, it appeared to be a typically traditional, elementary classroom. Yet something seemed different that day I entered it for the first time.

My job was to make classroom visitations and implementation of a training program that focused on language arts ideas that would empower students to feel good about themselves and take charge of their lives.

Donna was one of the volunteer teachers, who participated in this project. I took an empty seat in the back of the room and watched. All the students were working on a task, filling a sheet of notebook paper with thoughts and ideas.

The ten-year-old student next to me was filling her page with "I Can't." "I can't kick the soccer ball past second base." "I can't do long division with more than three numerals." "I can't get Debbie to like me."

Her page was half-full and she showed no signs of letting up. She worked on with determination and persistence. I walked down the row glancing at students' papers. Everyone was writing sentences, describing things they could not do.

By this time, the activity engaged my curiosity, so I decided to check with the teacher to see what was going on but I noticed she too was busy writing. I felt it best not to interrupt.

"I can't get John's mother to come for a teacher conference." "I can't get my daughter to put gas in the car." "I can't get Alan to use words instead of fists."

Thwarted in my efforts to determine why students and teacher were dwelling on the negative instead of writing the more positive "I Can" statements, I returned to my seat and continued my observations.

Students wrote for another ten minutes. They were then instructed to fold the papers in half and bring them to the front. They placed their "I Can't" statements into an empty shoebox.

Then Donna added hers. She put the lid on the box, tucked it under her arm, and headed out the door and down the hall. Students followed the teacher.

I followed the students. Halfway down the hallway Donna entered the custodian's room, rummaged around and came out with a shovel.

Shovel in one hand, shoebox in the other, Donna marched the students out to the school to the farthest corner of the playground. There they began to dig. They were going to bury their "I Can't"!

The digging took over ten minutes because most of the fourth graders wanted a turn. The box of "I Can't" was placed in a position at the bottom of the hole and then quickly covered with dirt.

Thirty-one ten and eleven year-olds stood around the freshly dug gravesite. At this point Donna announced, "Boys and girls, please join hands and bow your heads." They quickly formed a circle around the grave, creating a bond with their hands.

They lowered their heads and waited. Donna delivered the eulogy. "Friends, we gathered here today to honor the memory of 'I Can't.' While he was with us here on earth, he touched the lives or everyone, some more than others.

We have provided 'I Can't' with a final resting place and a headstone that contains his epitaph. He is survived by his brothers and sisters, 'I Can,' 'I Will', and 'I'm Going to Right Away'.

They are not as well known as their famous relative and are certainly not as strong and powerful yet. Perhaps some day, with your help, they will make an even bigger mark on the world than you did for anyone.

May 'I Can't' rest in peace and may everyone present pick up their lives and move forward in his absence. Amen." As I listened, I realized that these students would never forget this day. Writing "I Can't," burying it and hearing the eulogy.

That was a major effort on this part of the teacher. Moreover, she was not done yet. She turned the students around, marched them back into the classroom, and held a wake. They celebrated the passing of "I Can't" with cookies, popcorn, and fruit juices.

As part of the celebration, Donna cut a large tombstone from butcher paper. She wrote the words "I Can't" at the top and put RIP in the middle.

The date was added at the bottom. The paper tombstone hung in Donna's classroom for the remainder of the year. On those rare occasions when a student forgot and said, "I can't," Donna simply pointed to the RIP sign.

The student then remembered that "I Can't" was gone and chose to rephrase the statement. I was not one of Donna's students. She was one of mine. Yet that day I learned an enduring lesson from her as years later, I still envision that fourth grade class lying to rest, "I Can't."

For many of us, we have found times where we said to ourselves that we could not do something any more. It could be a job, a relationship, or feeling a certain way.

The truth is there are some things that you should not feel. You should not do some things. There are other things you do not need or want. It is okay to let it go, be it a feeling, an item, like a car, or even, a person.

As I mentioned before and we all have heard it, everyone comes into your life for a reason, season, or a lifetime. People come into your life for a specific reason, or a time or they may become a part of your life for the rest of your life.

When they are only there for a reason or season, you must learn to let go. Whenever something seems impossible, that is the moment you need to let God...

Letting God....

I have talked about letting go, letting in and letting God. I know you are probably wondering so how are you supposed to know what time you will have with that person. Trust me, you will not know. Something will often happen that will tell you when its' time to let somebody or something go.

Maybe, it is the bad feelings you have about them or the object. Remember that pain is often a sign that something is wrong like your finger hurting when it is cut. What if this person makes you feel uneasy? If being around this person hurts you, instead of making you feel better about yourself, let them go and let God deal with all else.

If this person makes you feel stuck in the past, then it is time to let go. You are an adult, but they treat you like a child. They still act as if you are still ten, instead of thirty, which you are now. Let them go.

I also learned to let go of anybody that brings any kind of negativity into my life. They are not going to stress me. I apologize. I am not sorry. We all know people like this who will call you up when they are having a bad day.

They will tell you everything about what is wrong to them.

They will always tell you how somebody did something to them and how they responded. The person should not have done X, Y, or Z to them. It is always about them.

Do they ever ask you about your day? Do they ask you about what you may be going through? On the other hand, they are the chronic complainer; they hate the world and everything in it? Do you ever think it might be them? You probably do, but never said it.

So with that said, let us get started. Breaking up is so hard to do. It is hard because again you have to admit you made a mistake. If the relationship was not good for you because maybe the person stopped being good to you and good for you, let them go.

Then, let God deal with it. God can mend even a broken heart, but first you have to give him all of the pieces, not just some of them. Letting go means letting God.

Your decision should always be based on what is best for you. Will the relationship continue to bring you problems, or will it bring you peace? You have to make a decision that brings peace within and around you.

It might be a "friend," who is really an associate, or it might be a co-worker. This person has harmed you and no apologies will work. They may have said that they would change, but they do not. They will never even try. When all else fails. Let them go.

What should be the best thing for you may feel like the end of the world. For some people bad relationships are often built around some form of dependency. You just cannot live without them. Just like a poor rat with only one hole to crawl into, you do not have anywhere else to go.

You become so emotionally attached that you feel like you have so much invested that you have to work harder to save it. The product of any bad situation is often your self-esteem. Remember you cannot base your happiness on the actions of others.

You should never allow your self-esteem or sense of one's self be lowered to satisfy the expectations of others, So let me ask you, if you and that person that is hurting you suddenly stopped speaking, are you better off without them or worst?

In a relationship, some people will actually tell their significant other that they will never find anybody better than them. When things go bad and they are the only one's there to prop you up, it sounds like the truth.

The key to letting go is to realize your worth with and without them. Know your strengths. Surround yourself with people that understand these things about you, because they will remind you of these things when you need it. That is a true friend.

My rule on letting people go in my life is the good-bad scale. When the bad outweighs the good on a ninety percent to ten percent scale, it is time to go. There will be time when people will be at the fifty-fifty scale and that little thing will tip the scale, based on how a person made you feel at that moment.

The one thing I never liked more than anything else is how a person tries to make people feel bad on purpose. They are not happy, why should you be?

Misery loves company. Some people can come into your life and truly make you feel better about yourself. Others, they can truly make you feel worst. Do not let them.

I know that a person can only do to you what you allow. However, love too can make you do some crazy things, when you love someone. For some people, that new person can make you feel like you can change the world and in the end, you only change yourself. Often, this change is for the worst.

I once knew somebody that told me I was too nice. I used to laugh. Too nice? Is there such a thing? I would later learn that they meant I treated them too nice. They expected the worst because their self-esteem was low.

What I soon learned that some people could not accept that you are nice to them. After so much anger and misery, they are afraid that your actions come with some kind of price tag. That should not always be the case, but for them, it is.

When you stop "associating" with someone who is not any good for you, there is something else you should do. Get rid of any daily reminders of them. Everything, if you can do just that. It will help you eventually.

Getting rid of reminders will help you do some thing very important; it helps you keep from backsliding. In an abusive situation, it often takes an abused woman seven times to walk away from her abuser.

In an abusive relation, there is often a period where he is good to her and these reminders might remind her of those good times. That little teddy bear might become his opportunity for her to let him back into her life. Do not rethink it. Do not mull over it. Let it go.

The same way that you feel like you should reunite with someone that you love, for some people, they feel that need to let somebody who is not good for them back in. So get rid of anything that will remind you of them.

If you cannot get rid of the reminders, at least put them away. Out of sight becomes out of mind. If you were living with the person, do yourself a favor and make the space your own. Move some furniture and paint the walls. If it is possible, just move.

As with anything, this process to get over them will take time. You owe it to yourself to be happy. You can do it. I know you can.

According to Lewis B. Smedes, "You will know that forgiveness has begun when you recall those who hurt you and feel the power to wish them well." With that said, now what?

The Final Secret To Your Well-Being

There is another secret that I feel, that you need to know. I have a firm belief that we all give our problems power. When bad things happen we often dwell on them so much we cannot focus on anything else.

Like the attention that we give our children to ensure that they grow up big and strong, we do the same things with our problems. That is why we need to be careful about our thoughts, because they will be come our words. Our words then tend to become our actions. Very few know and apply this secret.

The result? Millions of people are suffering undeserved stress, trials, problems, and heartache. They never seem to be a success in life. Bad days follow bad days. Terrible things seem to be constantly happening.

Theirs is constant stress, lack of joy, and broken relationships. Your worrying consumes time and the resulting anger will destroy your friendships. Life seems dreary and then, is not enjoyed to the fullest.

Friends are lost. Life is a bore and often seems cruel. Does this describe any part of you? If so, do not be discouraged. You can be different. It is the secret to forgiveness.

When you understand and apply this secret, it will change your life! What is this secret? It is the 90/10 rule. The first 10% of your life is made up of what happens to you. The other 90% of life is decided by how you react to it.

What does this mean? We really have no control over 10% of what happens to us. We cannot stop the car from breaking down. The plane may be late arriving, which throws our whole schedule off. A driver may cut us off in traffic. We have no control over this 10%.

The other 90% is different. You determine the other 90%! How? By your reaction! You cannot control a red light, but you can control your reaction. Do not let people fool you; YOU can control how you react!

Let us use an example. You are eating breakfast with your family. Your daughter knocks over a cup of coffee onto your business shirt. You have no control over what just happened. What happens next will be determined by how you react to it.

So what happened? You harshly scold your daughter for knocking the coffee cup over.

She breaks down in tears. After scolding her, you turn to your spouse and criticize your spouse for placing the cup to close to the edge of the table.

A short verbal battle follows this. You then storm upstairs and change your shirt. Back downstairs, you find your daughter has been too busy crying to finish breakfast and get ready for school. She misses the bus.

Your spouse must leave immediately for work. You rush to the car and drive your daughter to school. Because you are late, you drive 40 miles per hour in a 30 miles per hour speed limit zone.

After a 15-minute delay and throwing $60 (traffic fine) away, you arrive at school. Your daughter runs to the building without saying good-bye. After arriving at the office 20 minutes late, you find you forgot your briefcase. Bad day, huh?

Your day has started terrible. As it continues, it seems to get worse and worse. You look forward to going home. When you arrive home, you find a small wedge in your relationship with your spouse and daughter.

Why is that? Is it because of how you reacted in the morning? Why did you have a bad day?

A) Did the coffee cause it?

B) Did your daughter cause it?

C) Did the Policeman cause it?

D) Did you cause it?

The answer is D. You had no control over what happened with the coffee. How you reacted in those 5 seconds is what caused your bad day. Here is what could have and should have happened. Coffee splashes over you. Your daughter is about to cry.

You gently say, "It is okay, honey. I forgive you; you just need to be more careful next time." Grabbing a towel, you rush upstairs. After grabbing a new shirt and your briefcase, you come back down in time to look through the window and see your child getting on the bus. She turns and waves.

You and your spouse kiss before you both go to work. You arrive 5 minutes early and cheerfully greet the staff. Your boss comments on how good of day you are having. Did you notice the difference?

These are two different scenarios. Both started the same. Both ended different. Why, because of how you REACTED. You really do not have any control over 10% of what happens. The other 90% is determined by your reaction.

Here are some ways to apply the 90/10 secret. If someone says something negative about you, do not be a sponge. Let the attack roll off like water on glass.

You do not have to let the negative comment affect you! React properly and it will not ruin your day. A wrong reaction could result in losing a friend, being fired, being stressed out, etc.

How do you react if someone cuts you off in traffic? Do you loose your temper? You pound the steering wheel. (A friend of mine had the steering wheel fall off!)

Do you curse? Does your blood pressure skyrocket? Do you try to bump them? WHO CARES if you arrive ten seconds later at work? Why let the blue car ruin your drive?

Remember the 90/10 principle, and do not worry about it! You are then told that you lost your job. Why lose sleep or get irritated? It will work out. Use your "worrying" energy and time into finding another job.

The plane is late. It is going to mangle your schedule for the day. Why take out your frustration on the flight attendant? She has no control over what is going on.

Use your time to study, to get to know the other passengers, etc. Why are you getting stressed out? It will just make things worse. You now know the 90-10 secret. Apply it and you will be amazed at the results.

The 90/10 secret simply allow you to do what I have said and that is to forgive early and forgive often. It is not what happens to you but how you respond to it.

All that ever counts is love, prayer, and forgiveness. It is not what happens to you that matters most, but how you deal with it.

If you noticed, I have applied the 90/10 rule through out this entire book. Forgiveness is based on how you react to a slight or wrong and not what happens to you.

As it is written in Matthew 6:14, "For if you forgive men when they sin against you, your heavenly father will also forgive you…"

Epilogue

With each chapter in this book, I shared with you a story that reflected a topic within this book. Each time, I tried to move you closer to the moment that few will ever understand until now...true, if not total, forgiveness.

It is a powerful feeling having control like that over your life and problems. It is the true moment when even God stops keeping score. With true forgiveness comes closure and the first opportunity to move forward.

The truth is, bad things can and will happen to good people. Yet, rather than dwell on the pain and misery, it is becomes better to learn to forgive and move forward.

Forgiveness is possible for you and anyone who you truly feel deserves it, especially you.

The key is to learn how to forgive yourself first. It will not happen overnight though, but it can happen if you try. Without a test, there would not be a testament. This is yours.

I pray that for you that this journey be one of hope that your life can be better, not because you say it will be but because you worked to make sure that, it is.

When you need it, never be afraid to seek out help. Again, forgiveness is not based on what happens to you but how you respond it.

There will always be someone willing to help, if you need it. You must be willing to ask. Just remember, the key steps:

- Acknowledge what happened.

- Accept that you cannot change the past. What is done is done.

- Ask for forgiveness for yourself and forgive others. Be honest. Be sincere. Do it for yourself first.

- Then, be committed to the change that will come from moving forward.

When in doubt, forgive early and forgive often. Forgiveness is the final act of love. Stay blessed and I wish you the very best....

R.A. Clark

About The Author…

R.A. Clark is a gifted, award winning educator and life coach. With the sudden lost of his mother, and a father, who battled substance abuse, R.A. Clark understands adversity and challenges. R.A. Clark has used his past struggles to help others.

In a continued effort to give back, a portion of the proceeds from the sale of his work, including this book, will go to support various women and children charities. R.A. Clark currently lives with his family and works in Philadelphia, PA.

Resources:

Remember that we all need help at some point; the following is a list of national hotlines that may point you in the right direction when you are in need of support. Please use them:

Domestic Violence Help: 1-800-829-1122

Covenant House Hotline: 1-800-999-9999

Alcohol and Drug Abuse Helpline and Treatment: Call 1-800-234-0420

Youth Crisis Hotline: 1-800-442-4673

Alcohol Abuse and Crisis Intervention: Call: 1-800-234-0246

National Drug Information Treatment and Referral Hotline: 1- 800-662-HELP (4357)

24 Hour Parenting Hotline: 1-888-281-3000

National Mental Health Association: Call: 1-800-969-6642

CPSIA information can be obtained
at www.ICGtesting.com
Printed in the USA
LVOW12s2227170317

527581LV00001B/22/P